D1494629

AQA GCSE (9-1) Computer Science

S. Robson

P.M. Heathcote

Published by
PG Online Limited
The Old Coach House
35 Main Road
Tolpuddle
Dorset
DT2 7EW
United Kingdom
sales@pgonline.co.uk
www.pgonline.co.uk
2016

PG ONLINE

Acknowledgements

The answers in the Teacher's Supplement are the sole responsibility of the authors and have neither been provided nor approved by the examination boards.

We would also like to thank the following for permission to reproduce copyright photographs:

Server Room © Google/Connie Zhou

How Secure is My Password screenshot © RoboForm, Siber Systems, Inc

PayPal screenshot © PayPal Inc

Other photographic images © Shutterstock

Cover picture © 'Dawn Vista' 2015
Screenprint, 93cm x 91cm
Reproduced with the kind permission of Hetty Haxworth
www.hetty-haxworth.co.uk

Cover artwork, graphics and typesetting by PG Online Ltd

First edition 2016

Preface

This is a brand new book from two popular and experienced authors. Aimed at GCSE students, it provides detailed coverage of all the topics covered in the new AQA 8520 Computer Science specification, written and presented in a way that is accessible to teenagers. It can be used as a course text and as a revision guide for students nearing the end of their course.

It is divided into eight sections covering every element of the specification. Sections 1, 2A and 2B of the textbook cover algorithms and programming concepts with a theoretical approach to provide students with experience of writing, tracing and debugging pseudocode solutions without the aid of a computer. These sections would complement practical programming experience.

Each section contains in-text questions and practice exercises. Answers to all these are available to teachers only in a free Teachers' Pack which can be ordered from our website **www.pgonline.co.uk**.

Approval message from AQA

This textbook has been approved by AQA for use with our qualification. This means that we have checked that it broadly covers the specification and we are satisfied with the overall quality. Full details of our approval process can be found on our website.

We approve textbooks because we know how important it is for teachers and students to have the right resources to support their teaching and learning. However, the publisher is ultimately responsible for the editorial control and quality of this book.

Please note that when teaching the GCSE Computer Science course, you must refer to AQA's specification as your definitive source of information. While this book has been written to match the specification, it cannot provide complete coverage of every aspect of the course.

A wide range of other useful resources can be found on the relevant subject pages of our website: www.aqa.org.uk.

Contents

Section 1 – Fundamentals of algorithms

Objectives

- Understand and explain the term algorithm
- Understand and explain the term decomposition
- Understand and explain the term abstraction
- Use a systematic approach to problem solving and algorithm creation using pseudocode and flowcharts
- Use meaningful identifier names and know why it is important to use them
- Determine the purpose of simple algorithms
- Understand that more than one algorithm can be used to solve the same problem
- Compare the efficiency of algorithms, explaining how some algorithms can be more efficient than others in solving the same problem
- Understand and explain how the linear search algorithm works
- Understand and explain how the binary search algorithm works
- Compare and contrast the linear and binary search algorithms
- Understand and explain how the merge sort algorithm works
- Understand and explain how the bubble sort algorithm works
- Compare and contrast merge sort and bubble sort algorithms

1.1 Algorithms, decomposition and abstraction

What is an algorithm?

An **algorithm** is a series of steps that can be followed to complete a task. It is not the same thing as a computer program – before you can write the program you have to work out the steps needed to solve the given problem. Writing the code is the easy part; working out exactly what the code has to do is more difficult.

A working algorithm will always finish and return an answer or perform the task it was supposed to. "Always finishes" is something you may take for granted until you write a program that gets stuck in an infinite loop (always save before you run your program!).

Let's take a step back from programming for a moment. Other sorts of algorithm that you may be familiar with are:

- recipes
- directions
- knitting patterns
- instruction for flat-pack furniture

Here's a problem:

How do I get from the Winchester service station on the M3 to Winchester High Street?

An algorithm does not have to be written in code. The first steps to working out the design will be to draw diagrams and/or list the steps involved.

We will be looking at how to break down the problem and then structure a solution using some standard tools called **flow charts** and **pseudocode**.

Only when the solution has some structure can you effectively start coding it. Pseudocode is the first step to actual code as it outlines the algorithm in programming constructs but doesn't rely on any specific language syntax.

Winchester Services

› Get on M3

› Follow M3 to A272. Take exit 9 from M3

ⱴ Continue on A272. Take A31 to B3330

   At the roundabout, take the 1st exit onto A272

   At the roundabout, take the 2nd exit onto A31

   At the roundabout, take the 1st exit and stay on A31

   At the roundabout, take the 2nd exit onto Bar End Rd/B3330
   Continue to follow Bar End Rd

   Turn right onto Bar End Rd/B3330
   Continue to follow B3330
   Go through 1 roundabout

   At the roundabout, take the 1st exit onto Bridge St/B3330
   Continue to follow B3330

High St

Q1 Look at the following algorithm:

    x ← 0
    FOR n ← 1 TO 10
        ask user to enter a mark
        accept the mark
        IF mark > x THEN x ← mark
    ENDFOR
    display x

What does this algorithm display if the numbers 14, 7, 16, 12, 10, 18, 12, 9, 11, 8 are entered?

What would make this algorithm easier to understand?

Q2 Write an algorithm to add up the numbers 1 to 100.

Decomposition

When you started programming, your whole program fitted on the screen. It was really easy to see what was going on and fix the problems. As programs get much bigger they become unmanageable so we need to break them into smaller sections.

Decomposition involves the breaking down of a problem into smaller, simpler steps or stages. For example, imagine we are writing a computer game which has many complex levels. We could break it up as follows:

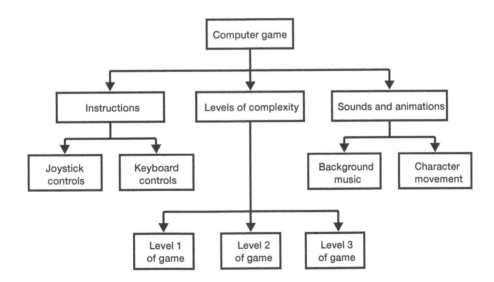

Each of the boxes could be further sub-divided until each box represents a single, simple sub-task. When tasks are broken down in this way, i.e. **decomposed**, it becomes much easier to solve the problem. Each small part of it is itself a small, manageable subproblem for which the steps in a solution can be written down.

Computational thinking

Computer Science is all about studying problems and figuring out how to solve them. The problem might be a mathematical one like adding the numbers 1 to 100, or finding all the prime numbers less than a million. Or, it might be something less well-defined, like getting a computer to recognise when the platform of an underground railway is becoming dangerously full. It could be a problem that a virus-checker attempts to solve – detecting when your computer has a virus.

A human being looking at a CCTV of an Underground platform would be able to tell quite easily if it was too crowded, and no more people should be allowed through the barrier. But how do we get a computer to recognise that situation?

Some of the key concepts in computational thinking include:

- abstraction
- decomposition
- algorithmic thinking

Abstraction

Abstraction involves removing unnecessary details from a problem in order to solve it. We are all familiar with the idea of abstracting away details from abstract paintings and statues; think of the famous statue "Angel of the North" by Anthony Gormley, dominating the skyline near the A1 at Gateshead.

How can this principle be applied to the problem of recognising a crowded platform? The computer needs to pick out the relevant objects and ignore the rest. It can ignore the background lights, the colour of the clothes people are wearing, whether they are carrying rucksacks and whether they are male or female. The only important fact is how many heads can be detected.

Q3 Can you think of any other way a computer could figure out whether a platform is overcrowded?

Is the presence of the train relevant?

Abstraction is used in thousands of different ways to aid in problem-solving. One common method of problem-solving is by using **simulation** – building a model of a problem and finding out what happens under different circumstances. Of course, it does not have to be a physical model; it is more likely to be what is termed a 'logical' model, that is, one which describes the basic facts and does a lot of calculations to help predict what will happen in different circumstances. Simulations of this sort include:

- weather and climate change models

- financial models like economic forecasts for governments or tools to calculate whether your business is likely to make a profit

- population models to help predict the likely population in 20 years' time, based on current trends

- queueing models, to help estimate how many toll-booths will be needed on a new motorway, or how many checkouts there need to be in a new supermarket

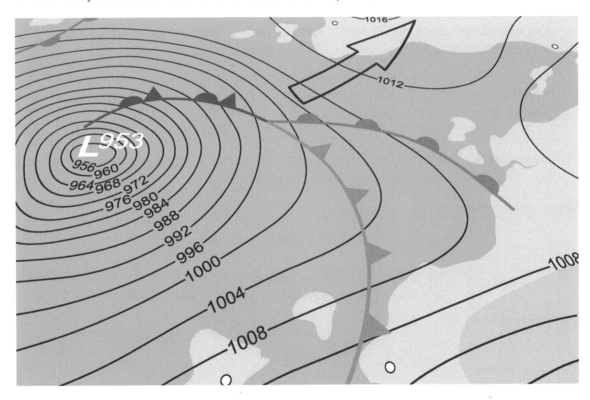

Q4 What would be the inputs to each of these models?
How is abstraction used in each case?

Abstraction allows us to separate the 'logical' from the 'physical'. A good example of this is the map of the London Underground – all we need to know is what stations are on which line, and the best route to get from A to B. There is no need to get bogged down in details of the exact distance between stations or even in which direction the route actually takes us at any given moment.

Similarly, we are all quite happy to use a computer or drive a car without having much idea of how it works. A driver, a child in the back seat and a mechanic all have a very different view of a car. We abstract away everything we don't need to know about and concentrate on the essentials.

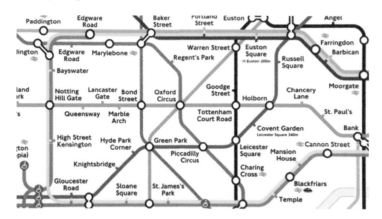

1.2 Developing algorithms using flowcharts

In computing we write programs or create computer systems to "solve a problem". The **problem** is the need or requirement we have to meet. The solution could be a simple program but is more likely to be a complex suite of hardware and software in a real-world scenario, which will need to be broken down into many programs and subroutines.

Understanding how to solve the problem is important. You cannot just start coding at line 1 and hope to get a working solution straight away. The first step is to write an **algorithm** – that is, the series of steps needed to solve the problem.

This section will consider how algorithms are developed with the aid of **flowcharts** and **pseudocode**. Flowcharts are diagrams which use certain symbols to show the flow of data, processing and input/output taking place in a program or task.

Standard flowchart symbols

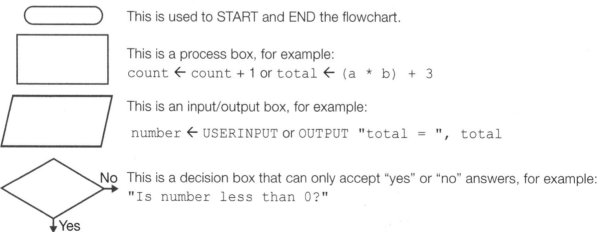

This is used to START and END the flowchart.

This is a process box, for example:
`count ← count + 1` or `total ← (a * b) + 3`

This is an input/output box, for example:

`number ← USERINPUT` or `OUTPUT "total = ", total`

This is a decision box that can only accept "yes" or "no" answers, for example:
`"Is number less than 0?"`

Example 1

In this flowchart, the value called `number` is continuously multiplied by 2 and the value is added to sum after each iteration of the loop.

The loop continues until the value of `sum` exceeds 29; at this point, `sum` is output.

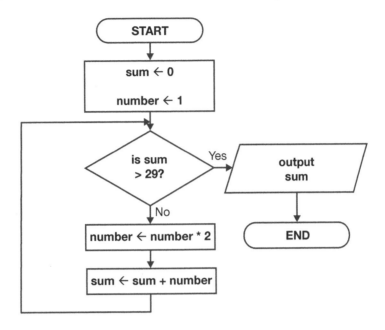

Q5 Complete the trace table to show how sum and number increase. What is output by the algorithm?

number	sum	sum > 29?
1	0	No

1

Using meaningful identifier names

In the flowchart above, we have used **identifiers** `sum` and `number` to refer to the **variables** used in the algorithm. Using meaningful identifier names is very important in helping someone looking at the algorithm to understand what it does and what each variable is used for.

It would be much harder to understand if we had used `x` and `y` as identifiers instead of `sum` and `number`.

You will see in the next question that the flowchart has deliberately been made more difficult to follow by using identifiers `temp1` and `temp2` instead of using names which explained what the variables hold. Can you think of more suitable identifiers?

Q6 The following flowchart inputs 365 temperatures and outputs the number of days when the temperature was more than 20°C and the number of days when the temperature was below 15°C. The average temperature for the 365 days is also output.

Give the statements that need to be inserted at A, B, C and D.

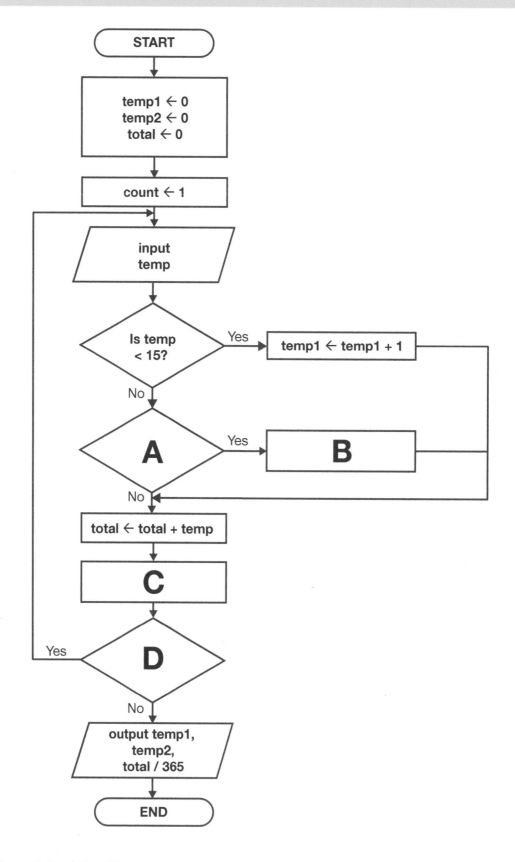

Q7 Draw a flowchart which inputs the top speed of a number of cars (-1 is used to stop the input). The average top speed of all the cars is finally output.

Q8 Draw a flowchart which outputs the maximum of 10 numbers input by the user.

1.3 Developing algorithms using pseudocode

Pseudocode is used to write an algorithm in programming-style constructs but it is not in an actual programming language. You do not need to worry about the detailed syntax or be precise about how the code will do something; you just describe the steps you will need in your algorithm.

Basic programming constructs

There are three constructs used to write algorithms in pseudocode (and in actual code):

- sequence
- selection
- iteration

Sequence

Sequence is just a matter of writing the steps down in the order they need to happen. For example:

```
Input the product price
Input the quantity
Calculate total ← quantity x price
Output "Total price is ", total
```

The statements above are perfectly acceptable pseudocode – it is quite clear what the steps are, and you can write your algorithms using similar statements. However, in an exam you will see more standardised pseudocode statements used, and the four statements above would be written as:

```
productPrice ← USERINPUT
quantity ← USERINPUT
total ← quantity * price
OUTPUT "Total price is ", total
```

Examples of pseudocode assignment statements

```
costPrice ← 10.0
total ← costPrice * 2
gender ← "M"
name ← "Mike Smith"
option ← True
```

Selection

Using an IF…THEN…ELSE statement

The `IF…THEN…ELSE` construct allows you to choose between two options.

```
IF x ≤ 10 THEN
   z ← z + 10
ELSE
   z ← z - 10
   y ← y + 1
ENDIF
```

Using an IF…THEN statement

You can write an `IF…THEN` statement without an `ELSE`.

```
IF gameWon = True THEN
        (instructions here)
ENDIF
```

Using an IF…ELSE IF statement

```
IF menuChoice = 1 THEN
   display rules
ELSE IF menuChoice = 2 THEN
   play game
ELSE IF menuChoice = 3 THEN
   exit
ENDIF
```

Nested selection statements

You can also write one or more `IF` statements nested inside another selection statement. The following example uses a nested `IF` statement.

Example 1

Write an algorithm to input a user name and check if it is equal to MANH123. If it is, input a user password, and check if the password is equal to XYZ123a, otherwise output a message "Invalid username". If the password is correct, output "Access granted", otherwise, output a message "Invalid password".

```
username ← USERINPUT
IF username = "MANH123" THEN
   password ← USERINPUT
   IF password = "XYZ123a" THEN
      OUTPUT "Access granted"
   ELSE
      OUTPUT "Invalid password"
   ENDIF
ELSE
   OUTPUT "Invalid username"
ENDIF
(continue)
```

Q9 Complete the nested IF statement below to check whether a variable called `element` is in either or both of two lists called `listA` and `listB`, and output an appropriate message

```
IF element in listA THEN
   IF element in listB THEN
      OUTPUT "Element is in both lists"
   ELSE
      OUTPUT "Element is in List A"
   ENDIF
ELSE
   (insert statements here)
   ...
```

Iteration

There are three basic iteration (loop) constructs that you will learn when you program.

FOR...ENDFOR loop

The FOR loop comes under the heading of **definite iteration**, which allows you to execute a group of steps a specific number of times.

```
FOR count ← 1 TO 10
   OUTPUT count * 3
ENDFOR
```

REPEAT...UNTIL loop

This loop is a form of **indefinite iteration**. It is a **condition controlled** loop which is controlled by a Boolean condition and will be repeated until this evaluates to True.

The condition could take the form `x = "End"`, `count = 10`, or `n > 100`, for example.

A REPEAT...UNTIL loop is a condition controlled loop in which the condition is tested *at the end* of the loop.

It will, therefore, always execute the following steps *at least once*. Here is an example of an algorithm that uses a REPEAT...UNTIL loop. This loop will be performed 10 times:

```
count ← 1
REPEAT
   OUTPUT count * 3
   count ← count + 1
UNTIL count > 10
```

WHILE...ENDWHILE loop

A WHILE...ENDWHILE loop is another type of **condition controlled** loop, repeated *while* a certain condition is true. The condition is tested *at the start* of the loop. It will, therefore, execute the following steps *zero or more* times. Here is an example of an algorithm that uses a WHILE loop:

```
x = USERINPUT
WHILE x ≠ "End"
   OUTPUT x
   x = USERINPUT
ENDWHILE
```

If the user inputs "End" before the WHILE statement, the loop will not be performed at all and execution will skip to the next statement after the ENDWHILE statement.

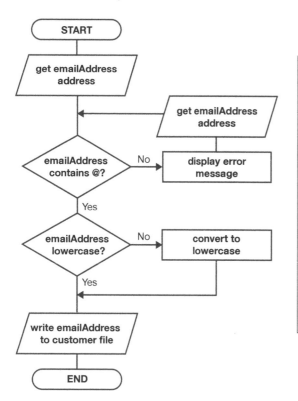

```
emailAddress ← USERINPUT

WHILE NOT hasAtSign
     OUTPUT error message
     emailAddress ← USERINPUT
ENDWHILE

IF emailAddress is not lowercase
THEN
     Convert to lowercase
ENDIF


write emailAddress to customer file
```

Example 2

A computerised form prompts a user to enter their email address.

The validation rules check if the address has an @ symbol in it. If it doesn't, an error message is displayed, the text box is cleared and the system asks the user to enter the email address again. This continues until an appropriate address is entered.

The system then checks that the email address has been typed in lowercase and if not, it converts it to lowercase. Once the email address is ok it is stored in the customer database.

The flowchart for this could be as follows:

Q10 The IF statement to check whether the address is lowercase is not needed. Modify the algorithm so that it performs the same task without using an IF statement.

Q11 Write a pseudocode algorithm which inputs 10 numbers. Each time a number less than zero is input, display which number it is, and its value. When all numbers have been input, display the average of all the negative numbers. Your algorithm should allow for the fact that there may be no negative numbers.

Sample output could be, for example

```
Number 3   -8
Number 7   -20
Average of negative numbers = -14
```

Q12 Write a routine that inputs a series of numbers. Output how many numbers are greater than 60. A dummy value of -1 ends the input.

1.4 Searching algorithms

Before starting to write algorithms for our own problems, we will look at some well-known algorithms for searching and sorting, which are both very common operations in the real world.

Thousands of software applications, including databases or commercial search engines such as Google, depend on the ability to quickly search through huge amounts of data to find a particular item.

 Q13 Name some other organisations that store huge amounts of data which often need to be searched quickly find a particular item.

We are going to consider two search algorithms in this section. Two of the most common search routines are:

- Linear search
- Binary search

A linear search

When the data is unsorted, the only sensible option when searching for a particular item is to start at the beginning and look at every item until you find the one you want. You could be lucky and find the item quite quickly if it's near the beginning of the list, or you could be unlucky and find it right at the end of the list.

 Q14 If you have a list of 10,000 unsorted names, on average how many items will need to be examined until you find the one you are looking for?

1

Here is an algorithm for a linear search:

```
1. found ← False
2. Start at the first name
3. REPEAT
4.    Examine the current name in the list
5.    IF it's the one you are looking for THEN
6.       found ← True
7.    ENDIF
9. UNTIL found = True OR reach end of list
9. IF found = True THEN
10.    OUTPUT name
11.ELSE
12.    OUTPUT "Not found"
13.ENDIF
```

The algorithm as written is a long way from something you can turn into program code, but it describes how you might go about solving the problem.

Example 3

Look at the following list of integers:

14	2	3	11	1	9	5	8	10	6

The items you would examine to find the number **5** would be: **14, 2, 3, 11, 1, 9, 5**

Q15 Write down the items you would examine to locate data item **7** in the above data list.

A binary search

If the list is sorted, (i.e. in numerical or alphabetical order), you can use a much more efficient algorithm called a binary search. It works by repeatedly dividing in half the portion of the data list that could contain the required data item. This is continued until there is only one item in the list you are examining.

This is the algorithm:

```
1. found ← False
2. REPEAT
3.    Examine the middle data item in the list
4.    IF this is the required item THEN
5.       found ← True
5.    ELSE
6.       IF required item > middle item THEN
7.          discard the first half of the list including middle item
8.       ELSE
9.          discard the second half of the list including middle item
10.      ENDIF
11.   ENDIF
12.UNTIL found = True OR there are no more items in the list
```

Example 3

Consider the following ordered list of 15 items. We want to find out whether the number 50 is in the list of 10 items.

| 15 | 21 | 29 | 32 | 37 | 40 | 42 | 43 | 48 | 50 | 60 | 64 | 77 | 81 | 90 |

Stage 1: The middle term is 43; we can therefore discard all data items less than or equal to 43.

| 48 | 50 | 60 | 64 | 77 | 81 | 90 |

Stage 2: The middle term is 64, so we can discard all data items greater than or equal to 64.

| 48 | 50 | 60 |

Stage 3: middle term is 50 – so we have found the data item.

Note that if there are an even number of items in the list, for example 8 items, the fourth, not the fifth, item is taken to be the middle item.

Q16 Suppose we have the following sorted list of 10 items:

| 3 | 5 | 6 | 8 | 11 | 12 | 14 | 15 | 17 | 18 |

Which one of the following is the correct sequence of comparisons when used to locate the data item 8?

    (i) 12, 6, 8   (ii) 11, 5, 6, 8   (iii) 3, 5, 6, 8   (iv) 11, 6, 5, 8

Q17 Ask a friend to think of a number between 1 and 1000. Then use a binary search algorithm to guess the number. How many different guesses will you need, at most?

Q18 Look at the following data list. Which items will you examine in (a) a linear search and (b) a binary search to find the following data items: 27, 11, 60?

9	11	19	22	27	30	32	33	40	42	50	54	57	61	70	78	85

Comparing linear and binary search algorithms

The linear search algorithm is fine for just a few items, but for a very large number of items, it is very inefficient. The average time taken to search 1000 items will be 100 times longer than the time taken to search 10 items. If you had to search a database of 10 million car registrations to find who owns a certain car, it would take a very long time.

In contrast, the binary search algorithm is extremely efficient. Each time an item is examined, if it is not the right one, half the list is discarded. In a list of 10 million items, only 24 items would need to be examined. That's because 10,000,000 is less than 2^{24}. In general, if there are fewer than 2^n items (but at least 2^{n-1}), the maximum number of items that needs to be examined is n.

A key benefit of the linear search is that it can be done on an unsorted list - the items do not have to be in sequence. If items are frequently added or deleted from the list, this saves the extra work needed to keep the list in sequence in order to do a binary search.

Q19 In the list of 17 items above, what is the maximum number of elements you would need to look at to find out if the element is in the list? Try searching for the number 9.

1.5 Sorting algorithms

In the last sub-section we looked at methods of searching for data. The binary search method required the data to be sorted before the search could take place. There are many algorithms for sorting data and we will look at two of them:

- Bubble sort
- Merge sort

Bubble sort

A bubble sort works by repeatedly going through the list to be sorted comparing each pair of adjacent elements. If the elements are in the wrong order they are swapped. A short algorithm to do the swapping is:

```
temp ← a
a ← b
b ← temp
```

If a = 9 and b = 6, the **trace table** below shows that the values of a and b have been swapped

temp	a	b
	9	6
9	6	9

Q20 Why could we not just write the two statements below to swap the values?

a ← b

b ← a

Example 4: Working through the Bubble sort algorithm

The figure below shows how the items change order in the first pass, as the largest item 'bubbles' to the end of the list. Each time an item is larger than the next one, they change places.

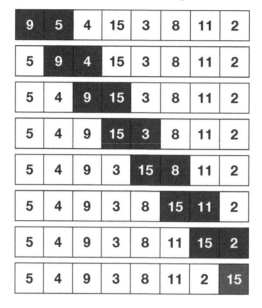

Pass 1

| 9 | 5 | 4 | 15 | 3 | 8 | 11 | 2 |

| 5 | 9 | 4 | 15 | 3 | 8 | 11 | 2 |

| 5 | 4 | 9 | 15 | 3 | 8 | 11 | 2 |

| 5 | 4 | 9 | 15 | 3 | 8 | 11 | 2 |

| 5 | 4 | 9 | 3 | 15 | 8 | 11 | 2 |

| 5 | 4 | 9 | 3 | 8 | 15 | 11 | 2 |

| 5 | 4 | 9 | 3 | 8 | 11 | 15 | 2 |

| 5 | 4 | 9 | 3 | 8 | 11 | 2 | 15 |

After the first pass as shown above, the largest item is in the correct place at the end of the list. On the second pass, only the first seven numbers are checked.

End of pass 2

| 4 | 5 | 3 | 8 | 9 | 2 | 11 | 15 |

11 and 15 are in the correct place; so only the first 6 numbers are checked.

End of pass 3

| 4 | 3 | 5 | 8 | 2 | 9 | 11 | 15 |

9, 11 and 15 are now in the correct place; so only the first 5 numbers are checked.

End of pass 4

| 3 | 4 | 5 | 2 | 8 | 9 | 11 | 15 |

8, 9, 11 and 15 are now in the correct place; so only the first 4 numbers are checked.

End of pass 5

| 3 | 4 | 2 | 5 | 8 | 9 | 11 | 15 |

5, 8, 9, 11 and 15 are now in the correct place; so only the first 3 numbers are checked.

End of pass 6

| 3 | 2 | 4 | 5 | 8 | 9 | 11 | 15 |

Finally, the first two numbers are checked and swapped

End of pass 7

| 2 | 3 | 4 | 5 | 8 | 9 | 11 | 15 |

The numbers are now in the correct order, and no further pass is required.

Algorithm for a bubble sort

In this algorithm, `numbers` is an **array** holding eight numbers. Each element of the array is referred to using an **index** in square brackets. In the array below, the first element of the array, 9, is held in `numbers[0]`, and the last element, 2, is held in `numbers[7]`.

Arrays are covered in Section 2A.4.

```
numbers ← [9, 5, 4, 15, 3, 8, 11, 2]
numItems ← len(numbers)       #get number of items in the array
FOR i ← 0 TO numItems - 2
   FOR j ← 0 TO numItems - i - 2
      IF numbers[j] > numbers[j + 1] THEN
            temp ← numbers[j]
            numbers[j] ← numbers[j + 1]
            numbers[j + 1] ← temp
      ENDIF
   ENDFOR
   OUTPUT numbers
ENDFOR
```

If you run this program, the output is

```
[5, 4, 9, 3, 8, 11, 2, 15]
[4, 5, 3, 8, 9, 2, 11, 15]
[4, 3, 5, 8, 2, 9, 11, 15]
[3, 4, 5, 2, 8, 9, 11, 15]
[3, 4, 2, 5, 8, 9, 11, 15]
[3, 2, 4, 5, 8, 9, 11, 15]
[2, 3, 4, 5, 8, 9, 11, 15]
```

Using a flag

Sometimes, a flag is tested on each pass so that if no swaps are made during a pass through the items, no more unnecessary passes are made through an already sorted list.

Suppose the list of numbers to be sorted is `[7, 2, 3, 4, 5, 8, 9, 11, 15]`

A variable called, for example, `flag` is set to `False` at the beginning of each pass. On the first pass, when a swap is made, `flag` is changed from `False` to `True`.

After the first pass, the numbers will be in the sequence `[2, 3, 4, 5, 7, 8, 9, 11, 15]` and are already in sequence.

On the second pass, as no swaps are made, `flag` remains `False`. This condition is tested, the loop ends and no more passes are made.

Here is the amended algorithm:

```
numbers ← [7, 2, 3, 4, 5, 8, 9, 11, 15]
numItems ← len(numbers)        #get number of items in the array
flag ← True                    #indicates when a swap is made
i ← 0
WHILE i < (numItems - 1) AND (flag = True)
   flag ← False
   FOR j ← 0 TO numItems - i - 2
      IF numbers[j] > numbers[j + 1] THEN
            temp ← numbers[j]
            numbers[j] ← numbers[j + 1]
            numbers[j + 1] ← temp
            flag ← True
      ENDIF
   ENDFOR
   i ← i + 1
ENDWHILE
OUTPUT numbers
```

This time, a flag is set to `False` at the beginning of each pass. As soon as a swap is made, the flag is set to `True`.

If a pass is completed without any swaps being made, the flag remains False and the `WHILE` loop ends. The sort is complete.

Q21 Carry out a bubble sort on the following set of numbers. The numbers are to be sorted in DESCENDING ORDER (highest to lowest).

| 6 | 8 | 1 | 17 | 27 | 11 | 15 | 3 | 14 | 42 | 5 |

(a) What is the order of the items after the first pass?

(b) (i) Using the simple bubble sort method which does not use a flag, how many passes through the data will be made?

(ii) What is the maximum number of passes on a list of 2 items?

(iii) What is the maximum number of passes on a list of 3 items? 10,000 items?

Merge sort

This is a two stage sort. In the first stage, the list is successively divided in half, forming two sublists, until each sublist is of length one.

Example 5: Sorting a list in ascending order

Stage 1

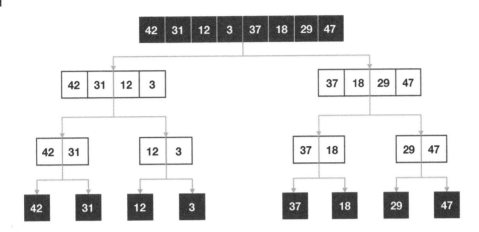

This is the end of stage 1 where all the elements have been separated out.

In the second stage, each pair of sublists is repeatedly merged to produce new sorted sublists until there is only one sublist remaining. As each pair of lists is merged, they are merged in order. Merging the final two sublists results in the sorted list.

Stage 2

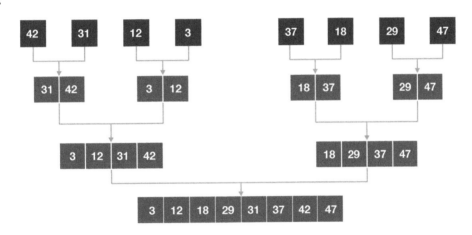

This is the end of stage 2, with all the items recombined in sorted order.

Q22 Carry out a merge sort on the following set of numbers. The numbers are to be sorted in ascending order.

| 6 | 8 | 1 | 17 | 27 | 11 | 15 | 3 |

(a) Write out the four sorted sublists after the first phase of Stage 2 (the merge process).

(b) Write out the two sorted sublists after the second phase of the merge process.

(c) Write out the complete list after the third phase of the merge process.

Q23 Which algorithm, the bubble sort or the merge sort, do you think is more efficient?

Comparing the merge sort and bubble sort algorithms

The bubble sort algorithm is very slow and inefficient for sorting more than a very few items. We saw that in a list of just eight items, seven passes through the data had to be made. On each pass, it is likely that some items will need to be swapped. You can imagine how long it would take to sort a million items using a bubble sort! Roughly speaking, to sort n items will need n^2 comparisons.

The merge sort, rather like the binary search, works by successively halving the data set. In this algorithm, this operation is repeated until each sublist is only one item long. Then the sublists are recombined. This is a much more efficient process than the bubble sort as it takes much less time to execute.

Its disadvantage for an inexperienced programmer is that it is a more difficult algorithm to implement. Another disadvantage is that it requires more memory to store the sublists, which can be a problem with a very large list.

Efficiency of algorithms

We have looked at two algorithms for searching a list, and two algorithms for sorting a list. In each case, either of the algorithms can be used to solve the problem, but one algorithm is much more efficient.

When performing a binary search, for example, doubling the size of the list from 1000 to 2000 items only involves halving the list one more time. Using a linear search, it could mean searching an extra thousand items!

Q24 Is a binary search always faster than a linear search? Explain your answer.

Many problems, both simple and complex, have more than one method of solution. Consider the problem of finding the sum of the integers from 1 to n. Here are two different algorithms for solving this problem.

Algorithm 1:

```
total = 0
FOR i = 1 TO n
   total = total + n
ENDFOR
```

Algorithm 2:

```
total = n*(n + 1)/2
```

The second algorithm is clearly much more efficient, as only one instruction is executed.

Q25 How many instructions are executed using each of the algorithms if n = 1000?

Exercises

1. **Abstraction** and **decomposition** are two aspects of computational thinking.

    (a) Sienna is designing a program to control a cat-flap which will open only when a cat belonging to the owner approaches.

    Describe two ways in which she may use abstraction in reaching a solution to this problem. [2]

    (b) A program is required to enter a set of students' examination marks, count the number of students who obtained each mark and output the counts for each mark. Examination marks entered must be in the range 0 to 100.

    Explain how **decomposition** might be used in designing a solution to this problem. [3]

2. (a) (i) A bubble sort is used to sort the following numbers in ascending order:

    34, 56, 89, 23, 12, 77, 49, 44

    What order will the numbers be in after the first pass? [2]

    (ii) How many passes will be required to sort the items? (No flag is used to indicate a sorted list.) [1]

    (b) A **merge sort** is to be used to sort the same numbers. During the merge phase, the following 4 pairs of numbers need to be merged into two groups of four.

    (34, 56), (23, 89), (12, 77), (44, 49)

    What will be the contents of each group of four numbers after the next phase of the merge? [2]

3. A list of surnames is held in sorted order. The names are:

    Beck, Coe, Ford, Grey, Hill, Kerr, Lunn, Pugh, Ross, Shaw, Taft, Ward

    (a) State which names would be examined when searching for the name **Grey** using

    (i) a linear search [1]

    (ii) a binary search [1]

    (b) State which names would be examined when searching for the name **James** using

    (i) a linear search [1]

    (ii) a binary search [1]

    (c) In a list of 1000 items, state the maximum number of names that would have to be searched to find a particular name using

    (i) a linear search [1]

    (ii) a binary search [1]

4. A school uses a computer program to give every new pupil a username for logging onto computers. The algorithm used to choose the username is shown below.

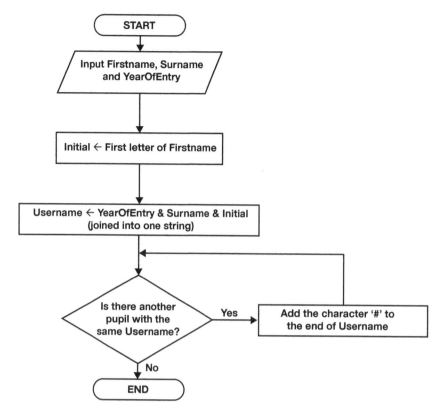

(a) Emily Smith joins the school in 2014. No other pupil called Smith joins the school in the same year.

State the username which Emily will be given and explain how you obtained your answer from the flowchart. [3]

(b) A pupil has the username 2013gillc##.

State four facts that you can work out from this username. [4]

5. A café sells three types of item:

iced bun	£1.50
cup cake	£2.00
muffin	£1.20

Write an algorithm using either a flowchart or pseudocode which:

inputs every item sold during the day

adds up the total amount taken for each item

outputs the total takings for each item

outputs the type of item that had the highest takings at the end of the day. [6]

6. Look at the flowchart below.

(a) Complete the trace table using the input data supplied and the headings given. [7]

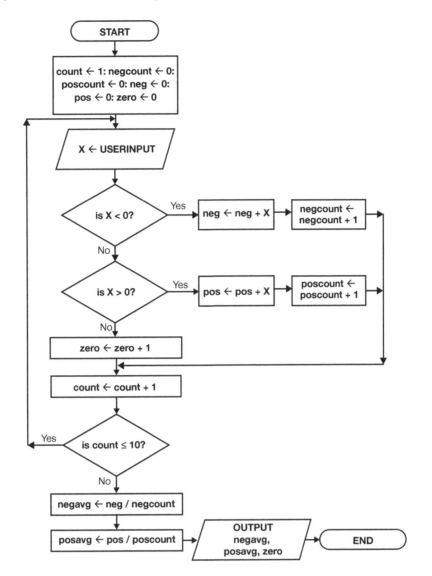

Input data: 0, 8, 7, 10, -8, -7, 0, 0, -3, 11

X	neg	negcount	pos	poscount	zero	count	count ≤ 10?	negavg	posavg	Output
0					1	2	Yes			
8			8	1		3	Yes			
7			15	2		4	Yes			
10			25	3		5	Yes			
-8	-8	1				6	Yes			
-7	-15	2				7	Yes			
0					2	8	Yes			
0					3	9	Yes			
-3	-18	3				10	Yes			
11			36	4		11	No	-6	9	-6, 9, 3

(b) What is the purpose of this algorithm? [3]

Section 2A – Programming basics

Objectives

- Understand and use data types: integer, real, Boolean, character and string

- Declare and use constants and variables

- Use input, output and assignment statements

- Use the common arithmetic operators including MOD and DIV

- Use relational operators $=$, $\neq$, $<$, $>$, $\leq$, $\geq$ and interpret them when used within algorithms

- Use the common Boolean operators AND, OR, NOT and combinations of these operators, within conditions for iterative and selection structures

- Use string handling and conversion functions

- Use definite and indefinite iteration

- Use nested selection and nested iteration statements

- Use one- and two-dimensional arrays

- Be able to use random number generation

- Use records to store data

- Read from and write to a text file

2A.1 Data types and operations

Variables and data types

Any data that a program uses must be stored in memory locations, each given its own **identifier** while the program is running. As the program runs, the values in these locations might change, which is why they are called **variables**. For example: a variable called `total` might change several times as many numbers are added to it. A variable called `surname` might change as a program processes a list of customer orders.

Each variable has an **identifier** (a unique name) that refers to a location in memory where the data item will be stored. Each variable also has a **data type** that defines the type of data that will be stored at the memory location and therefore the operations that can be performed on it (for example, you can multiply two numbers but you can't multiply two words).

Remember that it is important for the readability of the program to use meaningful identifier names – `total` rather than `t,` `surname` rather than `s`.

Declaring variables

In some programming languages variables are declared at the start of a program so that when the program runs, the appropriate amount of memory can be reserved to store the data. The following are examples from a Visual Basic program:

```
dim num1 as integer
dim total as single
dim choice as char
dim username as string
dim found as Boolean
```

In any high-level language where you declare variables, the statement will include an **identifier** and a **data type**.

In some languages, for example Python, variables are not declared at all. The program will assume the data type of a variable based on what is put in it. So if you write `a = 23, b = "Fred"`, a will be stored as an integer (whole number) and b will be stored as a string (text).

Even if you do not have to declare variables in your particular programming language, you need to understand the different data types and how to work with them in the programs you write.

The table below shows a list of some data types and the typical amount of memory that each needs.

Data type	Type of data	Typical amount of memory
integer	A whole number, such as 3, 45, -453	2 or 4 bytes
real/float	A number with a fractional part such as 34.456, -9.2, 4.10	4 or 8 bytes
char/character	A single character, where a character can be any letter, digit, punctuation mark or symbol that can be typed	1 byte
string	Zero or more characters. A string can be null (empty), just one character or many characters	1 byte per character in the string
Boolean	A Boolean variable has the value True or False	1 byte

2A

The programming language that you are using may have different names for some of these; for example, "real" is called "float" in some languages. Your language will also have some additional data types not listed. The amount of memory used for each data type varies for different programming languages too – for example, an integer may need two bytes in one language but four bytes in another.

Assignment statements

In most programming languages, values are assigned to variables using an = sign.
For example:

```
x = 1
pi = 3.142
alpha = "a"
street = "Elm Street"
over18 = True
```

In pseudocode, we will use the ← symbol to mean assignment, e.g. x ← 1

Constants

In some programs, there are certain values that remain the same (constant) while the program runs. The programmer could use the actual value in the code each time, but it is good practice to give the value a unique name (**identifier**) and then use that name throughout the program. Constants are declared at the start of a program and can then be referred to as needed in the code.

For example:

At the start of the program: `constant` **VATRate** ← 0.2

Later in the program code: `sellPrice` ← `netPrice` * **VATRate** + `netPrice`

Note, though, this does not mean that the constant's value will never change during the lifetime of the system! For example, the VAT rate will stay the same (constant) while the program runs in a shop each day but, after the next budget, it may change. The value allocated to that constant will then need to be edited in the program.

The two main benefits of declaring a constant are:

* When its value changes, you only have to edit it in one place rather than looking for every place in the program where you used that value

* The code will be easier to read and understand because the constant's identifier will be used instead of a number. This makes your code easier to debug and later on, maintain.

In some languages such as Python, there is no special way to declare constants at the start of the program. You just write an assignment statement such as

VATRATE ← 0.2

By convention, in Python the identifier (name) of a constant is written in uppercase, which makes it clear that this is a value which should not be changed within the code.

Input and output statements

Example 1

Write pseudocode for a program that asks the user to input their name. It should accept a name, for example `John` and then display `Hello John` on the screen.

```
OUTPUT "Please enter your name: "
myName ← USERINPUT
OUTPUT "Hello ", myName
```

The first statement displays on the screen

```
Please enter your name:
```

and waits for the user to enter something. If the user types `John`, the `OUTPUT` statement then displays on the screen:

```
Hello John
```

Operations on data

Operations are things you can do to specific types of data. For example, you can perform arithmetic operations on numbers and you can perform string-handling operations on text.

Numerical data types

Operations that can be performed on numerical data types are shown below.

Arithmetic operations	Comparison operations
(give a numerical result)	*(give a boolean result: True or False)*
eg: 25 + 3 = 28	eg: 456 > 34 is True

Arithmetic operations		Comparison operations	
+	(addition)	<	(less than)
-	(subtraction)	>	(greater than)
*	(multiplication)	≤ or <=	(less than or equal to)
/	(division)	≥ or >=	(greater than or equal to)
^	(exponentiation)		
DIV or //	(integer division)	≠, != or <>	(not equal to)
MOD or %	(modulus)	= or ==	(equal to)

The arithmetic and Boolean operators vary slightly between different programming languages. Where there are differences, the first option will be used in exam questions.

When performing operations on data items you need to consider the data types used. For example, in a simple calculation where two whole numbers are added together, variables could be defined as follows in Pascal:

```
var
    Num1, num2, total: integer;
```

But if the calculation involves division, then the answer variable should be declared as a real number because the result is unlikely to be a whole number:

```
var
    Num1, num2: integer;
    answer    : real;
```

The arithmetic operators `DIV` and `MOD` can only be performed on whole numbers (integers).

`DIV` is integer division. It works like normal division but returns the whole number of times one number goes into the other. Here are some examples:

```
13 DIV 3 = 4
30 DIV 3 = 10
32 DIV 3 = 10
```

`MOD` gives the remainder of integer division as follows:

```
13 MOD 3 = 1
30 MOD 3 = 0
32 MOD 3 = 2
```

The exponentiation operator calculates the power of a number, so for example $7^2 = 49$

> **Q1** State the values of w, x, y and z that will be output when these statements are executed:
>
> ```
> w ← 54
> x ← w MOD 7
> y ← x DIV 2
> z ← y^3
> OUTPUT w, x, y, z
> ```

String handling operations

Sometimes you need to change the type of a variable from a string to an integer or a real number, or vice versa. This is done with functions such as:

`STRING_TO_INT(StringExp)`	e.g. `STRING_TO_INT("45")`	evaluates to 45
`STRING_TO_REAL(StringExp)`	e.g. `STRING_TO_REAL("72.5")`	evaluates to 72.5
`INT_TO_STRING(IntExp)`	e.g. `INT_TO_STRING(21)`	evaluates to "21"
`REAL_TO_STRING(RealExp)`	e.g. `REAL_TO_STRING(3.142)`	evaluates to "3.142"

Note the use of quotation marks here denotes a string.

Changing a string to an integer in Python

Python, for example, accepts all user input as strings, not numbers. You may need to convert a string to a number so that you can use it in a calculation.

Consider the following program in Python:

```
num1 = input()
num2 = input()
num3 = num1 + num2
print("The sum is ", num3)
```

If the user enters the numbers 3 and 5, you would expect `num3` to be 8. However, the program outputs:

```
The sum is 35
```

What has happened? The numbers are input as strings, and the + symbol when used with strings means **concatenation**, or joining the two strings together. (Concatenation is discussed in more detail on the next page.)

You need to convert each of the strings to integers or floating point numbers. A corrected program would look like this:

```
num1 = int(input())
num2 = int(input())
num3 = num1 + num2
print("The sum is", num3)
```

In Python, the int function changes the variable type to an integer. This is called **casting**.

String manipulation

A string is a sequence of characters enclosed in quote marks. Programming languages have built-in **functions** to manipulate strings.

The functions given below are given in the pseudocode which will be used in an exam. Each programming language will have its own particular functions and syntax.

To get the length of a string:

```
LEN(stringExp) e.g. LEN("Elephant Shrew") evaluates to 14
```

To get a substring:

```
SUBSTRING(startPos, endPos, stringExp)
e.g. SUBSTRING(2, 4, "Mongoose") evaluates to "ngo"
```

(It is assumed on this course that a string starts at position 0, not 1, so `stringExp[0]` contains the first character of a string called `stringExp`, or `'M'` in the case of `Mongoose` above.)

To find the position of a character in a string:

```
POSITION(stringExp, char)
e.g. POSITION("crocodile", d) evaluates to 5
```

Q2 Write pseudocode statements to input a firstname and surname as a string, for example "Thomas Edison" and then use string manipulation functions to convert this to an initial and surname and output, for example, "T Edison".

Concatenation

Concatenation means "joining together".

Example 2

In the statements below, the result of each operation is shown in a **comment** on the right. In the pseudocode that we will be using, all comments will start with the character #.

```
firstname ← "Simon"
surname ← "Robinson"
fullname ← firstname + " " + surname      # "Simon Robinson"
n ← LEN(fullname)                         # 14
positionOfspace ← POSITION(fullname, " ") # 5
```

Q3 Write pseudocode to assign a 7-digit number to an integer variable. Convert this to a string, and output the middle three digits.

Converting characters to and from ASCII

ASCII stands for "American Standard Code for Information Interchange". Using this code, every character can be represented as a 7-bit binary pattern, allowing 128 different characters to be represented.

For example, "A" is represented by `1000001`, the same binary code as the decimal number 65. "B" is 66, "C" is 67,... "Z" is 90. (See Section 3.3.)

```
CHAR_TO_CODE("A") evaluates to 65
CODE_TO_CHAR(66) evaluates to "B"
```

 Write pseudocode statements to accept an uppercase character from the user, and output the next character in the alphabet. If the user inputs Z, the letter A should be output.

2A.2 Sequence and selection

In Section 1 the basic program structures of sequence, selection and iteration were briefly covered. In this section the use of these structures will be looked at in more detail, with examples of more complex algorithms.

Sequence

All programs have a series of steps to be followed in sequence. Here is an example in which the steps are simple assignment statements:

Example 3

```
OUTPUT "Enter score for Round 1: "
score1 ← USERINPUT
OUTPUT "Enter score for Round 2: "
score2 ← USERINPUT
averageScore ← (score1 + score2) / 2
OUTPUT "The average score is ", averageScore
```

Sometimes the sequence may be a series of calls to different subroutines which perform different tasks. Subroutines (functions and procedures) will be covered in Section 2B.1.

Selection

Before looking at algorithms using the different selection statements available in a programming language, we need to take a closer look at Boolean data types and expressions, since these are used to determine which path through the program will be taken.

Boolean data type

Boolean variables are either **True** or **False**. It makes no sense to perform mathematical operations on them or to compare them to see which is greater. With Boolean variables we use **logical operators** to create **Boolean expressions**. Suppose that A represents some condition, for example x ≤ 10, or speed > 30. Logical operations AND, OR and NOT may be used in Boolean expressions, where:

NOT: If A is True, then NOT A is False

AND: If A is True and B is True, then (A AND B) is True, otherwise (A AND B) is False

OR: If either or both of A and B is True, then (A OR B) is True, otherwise (A OR B) is False

Boolean expressions

Boolean expressions are used to control selection statements. For example:

```
IF speed > 30 THEN
   OUTPUT "Control your speed"
ENDIF
```

A complex Boolean expression contains one or more of the operators **AND**, **OR** or **NOT**. For example:

```
IF (X ≤ 10) OR (CurrentCharNum > LengthOfString) THEN …
IF (NOT((A = B) AND (A = C))) THEN OUTPUT "Sides not equal"
```

 Q5 Write pseudocode statements to check whether a username entered by the user is equal to either "User1" or "User2". If so, print "Access granted", otherwise print "Access denied".

Nested selection statements

Using a complex Boolean expression is often clearer than using a nested selection structure.

Example 4

Consider an estate agent's program that searches through a file of house details to find ones that match a customer's requirements. In this case the customer wants a house or flat, but it must have more than three bedrooms.

Using a nested IF statement we could write:

```
IF Rooms > 3 THEN
   IF type = "House" THEN
     Output details
   ELSE IF type = "Flat" THEN
     Output details
   ENDIF
ENDIF
```

It is shorter and clearer to write:

```
IF (Rooms > 3) AND ((type = "House") OR (type = "Flat")) THEN
   Output details
ENDIF
```

Notice the extra set of brackets around the second half of the expression. AND takes precedence over OR so without the extra brackets the program would return all the houses with more than three bedrooms as well as any flats, whether they have more than three bedrooms or not.

Writing robust code

Robust code is code which will not result in the program crashing due to an unexpected user input. The pseudocode below would crash for some inputs. Why?

```
num1 ← USERINPUT
num2 ← USERINPUT
OUTPUT num1/num2
```

2A

The algorithm needs to be amended so that it will not crash whatever the user enters.

```
num1 ← USERINPUT
num2 ← USERINPUT
IF (num2 = 0) THEN
    OUTPUT "Cannot divide by 0"
ELSE
    OUTPUT num1 / num2
ENDIF
```

Example 5

A room is to be carpeted using carpet that is 4m wide. The program asks the user to enter the room dimensions, and if the width is greater than 4, outputs "Carpet not wide enough". Otherwise, it calculates the length of carpet required by adding 5% to the length of the room.

The following algorithm has been written:

```
roomLength ← USERINPUT
roomWidth ← USERINPUT
IF roomWidth > 4 THEN
    OUTPUT "Carpet not wide enough"
ELSE
    carpetLength ← roomLength * 1.05
    OUTPUT "Length of carpet required = ", carpetLength
ENDIF
```

The algorithm could still give the wrong answer if the user entered a width greater than 4, and a length less than the width, as it assumes that the user always enters the shortest dimension as the width. The program needs to check for this. Here is the rewritten algorithm:

```
roomLength ← USERINPUT
roomWidth ← USERINPUT
IF (roomWidth > 4) AND (roomLength < roomWidth) THEN
    temp ← roomLength
    roomLength ← roomWidth
    roomWidth ← temp
ENDIF
IF roomWidth > 4 THEN
    OUTPUT "Carpet not wide enough"
ELSE
    carpetLength ← roomLength * 1.05
    OUTPUT "Length of carpet required = ", carpetLength
ENDIF
```

> **Q6** How much carpet does the algorithm calculate is required if the user enters:
> (a) a length of 2 and a width of 4?
> (b) a length of 3 and a width of 5?

Q7 In Section 1, you learned how to write complex selection statements using a nested `IF` statement

Write an algorithm to solve the following problem.

- If a student gets A* in GCSE Maths, he or she will be advised to consider taking Further Maths at A Level
- If a student gets A in GCSE Maths, he or she will be advised to consider taking Maths at A Level
- If a student gets B in GCSE Maths, he or she will be advised to consider taking Maths at AS Level
- Otherwise, they will be advised not to continue with Maths.

Q8 Julie has written an algorithm in the form of a flowchart for a dice game played with three dice. When the player rolls the dice, they are given points according to the rules shown in the flowchart.

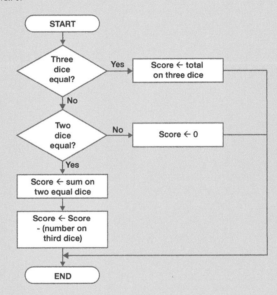

(a) Show the value of the score if the dice rolled are: (i) 2 4 6   (ii) 5 5 5   (iii) 2 2 3

(b) State a set of numbers which will result in a negative score.

(c) Write a selection statement which will test if all three dice are equal.

2A.3 Iteration

Frequently, sections of code need to be repeated a certain number of times, or until a certain condition is true or false.

`FOR...ENDFOR`, `WHILE...ENDWHILE` and `REPEAT...UNTIL` are three different types of iterative statement. Note that they are not always all available in a given programming language.

The FOR...ENDFOR loop

The `FOR...ENDFOR` loop is an example of **definite iteration**, meaning that the number of times the loop is to be repeated is defined. This type of loop is useful when you know how many times the loop is to be repeated.

For example, if you are drawing a square on a screen using a turtle, you could use the following algorithm:

```
FOR n ← 1 TO 4
   draw line
   turn 90 degrees
ENDFOR
```

Example 6

Suppose you need to write an algorithm which gives a user exactly three attempts to enter their password correctly. Assume the computer has the correct password in a variable called `correctPassword`.

A first go at writing the algorithm might be:

```
accessGranted ← False
FOR attempt ← 1 TO 3
   OUTPUT "Please enter password: "
   password ← USERINPUT
   IF password ≠ correctPassword THEN
      OUTPUT "Incorrect password"
   ELSE
      accessGranted ← True
   ENDIF
ENDFOR
```

Q9 How many times will the loop be performed if the user enters the correct password on the first attempt?

The problem with this algorithm, as you probably spotted, is that even if the user enters the correct password on the first attempt, they are still asked to enter it again a second and third time. A corrected algorithm is given in Example 7 below.

The WHILE…ENDWHILE loop

The `WHILE…ENDWHILE` loop is an example of **indefinite iteration**, in which the number of times the loop will be repeated depends on the loop condition being True. As soon as it becomes False, the loop terminates.

The expression in the `WHILE` statement controlling the repetition must be a Boolean condition which evaluates to True or False

The expression is tested at the **start** of the loop

This means that sometimes the statements inside the loop are not executed at all.

Boolean expressions are used to control this type of loop. For example:

```
WHILE reply ≠ "compScience"
   OUTPUT "Please re-enter password"
   reply ← USERINPUT
ENDWHILE
```

You may sometimes need complex Boolean expressions, for example:

```
WHILE (NOT A > B) AND (NOT ItemFound)...
```

Example 7

We can rewrite the algorithm given in Example 6 using a WHILE loop to allow the user up to three attempts.

```
accessGranted ← False
OUTPUT "Please enter password: "
password ← USERINPUT
attempt ← 1
WHILE (attempt ≤ 3) AND (accessGranted = False)
   IF (password ≠ correctPassword) THEN
      OUTPUT "Incorrect password - please re-enter: "
      password ← USERINPUT
      attempt ← attempt + 1
   ELSE
      accessGranted ← True
   ENDIF
ENDWHILE
```

A WHILE...ENDWHILE loop is also useful when allowing a user to continue entering data until they indicate there is no more data to enter by inputting a 'dummy' value. Here is an algorithm which allows a user to continue entering values until a dummy value of "xxx" is entered.

```
total ← 0
OUTPUT "Please enter next mark, xxx to end: "
markstring ← USERINPUT
WHILE markstring ≠ "xxx"
   mark ← STRING_TO_INT(markstring)
   total ← total + mark
   OUTPUT "Please enter next mark, xxx to end: "
   markstring ← USERINPUT
ENDWHILE
OUTPUT "Total of all marks: ", total
```

> **Q10** Write an algorithm which allows a user to enter daily temperatures and when the user enters -100, outputs the maximum and average temperature.

REPEAT...UNTIL loop

This is a second example of **indefinite iteration**. It differs from the WHILE...ENDWHILE loop in that it tests the loop condition at the **end** of the loop rather than at the beginning. It is therefore always performed at least once.

You may have seen pseudocode using a repeat loop to carry on until the user typed "N". The loop would look something like this with the condition at the end:

```
REPEAT
...
UNTIL continue = "N"
```

> **Q11** The statement x ← RANDOM_INT(1, 10) generates a random number between 1 and 10 and assigns it to x. Write a statement to generate a random score between 50 and 69.

Example 8

Write a program which tests someone on powers of 2 up to 2^{12}.

```
REPEAT
   power ← INT(2,12)
   powerOf2 ← 2 ^ power
   OUTPUT "What is 2 to the power of ", power
   answer ← USERINPUT
   IF answer = powerOf2 THEN
      OUTPUT "Correct, well done"
   ELSE
      OUTPUT "No, it is ", powerOf2
   ENDIF
   OUTPUT "Another go? Answer Y or N: "
   anotherGo ← USERINPUT
UNTIL anotherGo = "N"
```

Q12 Rewrite this algorithm using a WHILE...ENDWHILE loop.

Nested iteration

You can have one loop nested inside another.

Example 9

This algorithm displays all the multiplication tables between 2 and 12.

```
FOR table ← 2 TO 12
   FOR count ← 1 TO 12
      product ← table * count
      OUTPUT table, " x ", count, " = ", product
   ENDFOR
ENDFOR
```

Q13 What will be the third line output by this algorithm?

Q14 Write pseudocode for an algorithm which inputs the maths marks for the 30 students in each class in a school. There are 20 maths classes in the school.

Output the average mark for each class of 30 students (20 outputs) and the average mark for ALL of the students in the school.

2A.4 Arrays

We have said that all the variables needed in a program are held in main memory. If we were processing one or two specific data items, then we would have a variable for each of these. For example, a program that adds two numbers together might use variables called `num1`, `num2` and `total`, all of type integer.

Often a program will process a number of data items of the same type, for example if it is sorting a list of 1000 student names.

We could use variables called `student1`, `student2`, `student3`, ... `student1000` to store the names but programming languages allow you to use an **array** (or list) to make processing groups of data easier to code. An array is a group of data items of the same data type, which is stored under one identifier (name) in contiguous (one after another) memory locations.

1-dimensional arrays

This program processes 12 numbers using a simple array of integers called score. Imagine a table with one row of 12 boxes:

	0	1	2	3	4	5	6	7	8	9	10	11
score:												

Each box in the table can contain an integer. Each box has a numerical reference called a **subscript** or **index** that is used to refer to that individual data item. Note that the first element of the array shown here has a subscript of zero. For example, the third box in this array is referred to as `score[2]`.

In some languages the subscript starts at 1, and at the start of a program the array is defined, just as you would a variable. In Delphi, the array index could start at 0 or 1, so you could have:

```
score: array [1..12] of integer;
```

However, in the pseudocode used in this book, all arrays will have subscripts starting at 0.

The individual boxes in the array can be used just like variables:

- **Assign** values to them:

    ```
    score[4] ← 27
    ```

- **Input** values into them from the keyboard or a file:

    ```
    score[4] ← USERINPUT
    ```

- **Output** the value stored in a box to the screen or a file:

    ```
    OUTPUT "The fourth value is ", score[3]
    ```

The benefits of using arrays are:

- Code is easier to follow and therefore easier to debug and maintain

- A group of data items can be easily processed using a FOR loop

When you process data held in an array, you typically do the same thing to each data item, so having them stored in numbered locations makes this much easier and quicker to code.

Example 10

The following algorithm gets 12 numbers from the user, adds them up and outputs the total:

```
total ← 0
FOR game ← 0 TO 11
    score[game] ← USERINPUT
    total ← total + score[game]
ENDFOR
OUTPUT "Total is ", total
```

Q15 Write an algorithm which inputs ten names into an array, sorts them into alphabetical order and prints them out. You may assume that a method sort exists which will sort an array into ascending order. The statements

```
oldList ← [6, 4, 9, 24, 36, 1, 4]
newList ← oldList.sort()
```

will make `newlist` equal to [1, 4, 4, 6, 9, 24, 36]

Random number generation

It is often useful, especially in games programming, to generate a random number. For example, suppose you want to simulate throwing a six-sided die.

```
x ← RANDOM_INT(1,6)
```

will generate a random number between 1 and 6.

Example 11

Write a pseudocode algorithm which simulates throwing a six-sided die 1000 times. An array called `face[1..6]` is to hold the number of times each number (between 1 and 6) is thrown. Print out the number of times each number is thrown.

```
face ← [0, 0, 0, 0, 0, 0]
#throw die 1000 times and accumulate totals
FOR throw ← 1 TO 1000
    number ← RANDOM_INT(1,6)
    face[number] ← face[number] + 1
ENDFOR
#output the totals for each face
FOR n ← 1 TO 6
    OUTPUT face[n]
ENDFOR
```

Q16 Amend the program so that the array `face` starts at index 0, i.e. the array is `face[0..5]`

2-dimensional arrays

Suppose you needed to store 10 test scores for each of a class of 30 students. You could use a 2-dimensional array called `classScores`, which would, for example, hold the 8th test score for the 15th student in `classScores[14,7]`.

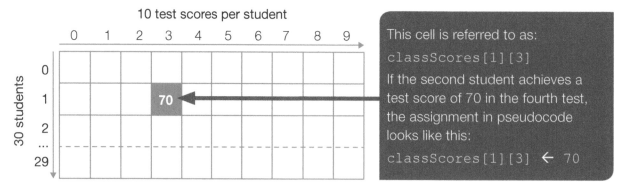

10 test scores per student

This cell is referred to as:
`classScores[1][3]`
If the second student achieves a test score of 70 in the fourth test, the assignment in pseudocode looks like this:
`classScores[1][3] ← 70`

Example 12

Write an algorithm to allow the user to enter the 10 test scores for each student, and calculate and output the average mark obtained by each student.

The student names are held in an array `studentName[0..29]` so that for example `student[0]` contains the name `Adams J`.

An array `total[0..29]` will hold the total mark for each student.

An array `average[0..29]` will hold the average mark for each student.

The program prompts the user: `"Enter 10 marks for Adams J"` and then stores the marks input by the user.

```
# initialize array to hold total marks
FOR n ← 0 to 29
    total[n] ← 0
ENDFOR
#input names and marks
FOR n ← 0 TO 29
    OUTPUT "Enter marks for ", studentName[n]
    FOR mark ← 0 TO 9
        classScores[n][mark] ← USERINPUT
        total[n] ← total[n] + classScores[n][mark]
    ENDFOR
ENDFOR
FOR n ← 0 TO 29
    average[n] ← total[n] / 10
    OUTPUT studentName[n], average[n]
ENDFOR
```

Q17 Write an algorithm which allows a user to enter a student number, and which then outputs their name, each of their 10 scores and their average score. You may assume the data for each student has been entered into the arrays using the algorithm given above.

Remember that the array indices start at 0, but the students will be numbered 1 to 30 in the teacher's record book. So if the teacher enters 3 for the student number, that student's name will be found in `studentName[2]` in the program.

Q18 Quarterly sales (in £000s) for each of six supermarkets are held in a two-dimensional array sales which has 6 rows and 4 columns. Write an assignment statement to assign the value 150 to Store 5 for the third quarter sales.

2A.5 Records and files

Earlier in the section we looked at arrays. An array is a collection of data items stored under one identifier so that the data items can be processed easily. When we group data items together so they can be treated as a set of data, we refer to this as a **data structure.**

The pseudocode programs we have looked at so far have all used variables which are stored in memory. Often, however, the data needs to be stored in a **file** which can be held permanently on disk, from where it can be read next time it is needed.

Records

Most languages will allow you to define arrays quite easily but sometimes we want to define our own data structures. Imagine a program for a car sales showroom. If your program is going to process details about cars, it will be easier to create a **record** structure to hold all of the car details rather than storing them as one long string of text or lots of separate variables. We cannot put them in an array because the separate data items we need to store about each car are not all of the same data type.

Here is a text file with some car details in it:

```
RE09 HSD,  Ford,      2012,   45000,  7000
SW12 SDF,  Vauxhall,  2005,   94000,  900
BN59 WJR,  Nissan,    2016,   4000,   12500
```

We could process this file as lines of text but it would be easier if we defined our own data type that gave this line of text some structure. In Delphi a programmer could define this **record** type as follows:

```
TYPE TCar = RECORD
   regNum: string[8];
   make: string[15];
   year: integer;
   mileage: integer;
   price: integer;
END;
VAR Car1: TCar;       # Car1 is a variable of type TCar
```

Individual data items within a record are called **fields**. The price of a car in a variable `Car1`, for example, can be referred to as `Car1.price`.

A typical algorithm to process all the records in a file will have the following steps:

```
WHILE NOT end of file
   read a record
   process the record
ENDWHILE
```

In a database, records are shown in a table like the one below, with each row representing a record for one car. Holding the data in this form makes it easy to add or delete a record, and to search for a car of a particular make, price, etc.

Registration	Make	Year	Mileage	Price
AV60 HES	Peugeot	2012	33156	£5,500
GF56 RTE	Toyota	2013	26875	£8,500
FD14 YOU	Hyundai	2011	85300	£3,499
AD45 HGF	Peugeot	2012	50887	£7,649
AF56 HTE	Peugeot	2013	45860	£6,780
GF59 NGB	Renault	2014	38665	£6,199
GR12 JUL	Renault	2011	90760	£2,999

Handling text files

Text files contain text that is in lines. There is no other structure, unlike files of records.

In many programming languages, you will need to follow these steps to access data in the text file:

1. Tell the program where the file is

2. Open the file to read from it (opens the file with a pointer pointing to the first line)

3. Read a line/lines of text from the file (this will automatically move the pointer down to the next line)

4. Close the file.

Writing to the file follows the same idea:

1. Open the file to write to

2. Write each line of text to the file one at a time, until there is no more text to write (note that writing is done at the end of the file)

3. Remember to close the file at the end.

Example 13: Writing to a file

In this example we will ask the user to input a list of names, and write them in a text file.

```
namefile ← OPENWRITE("names.txt")
WHILE name ≠ "xxx"
   OUTPUT "Please enter name"
   name ← USERINPUT
   namefile.writeline(name)
ENDWHILE
namefile.CLOSE
```

In the above version of the program, the dummy record "xxx" will be written to the file. If you don't want that to happen, you need to arrange for the read statement to be the last statement in the loop, so that the loop condition is tested immediately after reading.

```
namefile ← OPENWRITE("names.txt")
name ← USERINPUT "Please enter name"
WHILE name ≠ "xxx"
   namefile.WRITELINE(name)
   OUTPUT "Please enter name"
   name ← USERINPUT
ENDWHILE
namefile.CLOSE
```

Example 14: Reading from a file

Now the names are stored on the file, we can read them back and print them out, or store them in an array where they could, for example, be sorted alphabetically. In this example, there is no 'dummy' name at the end of the file.

```
namefile ← OPENREAD("names.txt")
WHILE NOT end of file
    name ← namefile.READLINE()
    OUTPUT name
    name ← namefile.READLINE()
ENDWHILE
namefile.CLOSE
```

Example 15: Reading records into an array

In this example, we will assume that the file of names has exactly 10 records.

```
namefile ← OPENREAD("names.txt")
n ← 0
WHILE NOT end of file
    name[n] ← namefile.READLINE()
    n ← n + 1
ENDWHILE
namefile.CLOSE
```

Q19 Write pseudocode for a procedure which allows the user to input the daily maximum temperatures for a week, and write them to a text file.

Comma-separated value files

Text files can contain more complex data and sometimes you will see **comma separated value** files that attempt to structure the line of text into fields, a bit like fields in a record of a database. The filename will have the suffix **.csv** but it is still essentially a text file. You still have lines of text, the only difference is that commas separate each field. Some programs will recognise this format and interpret it as separate data items on a line. Spreadsheets will do this. Here is a csv file with more students' scores in it.

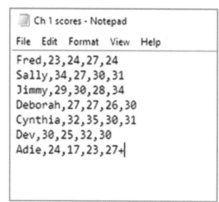

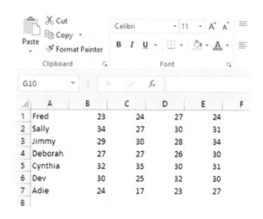

Viewed in notepad, as a text file   *How it looks if you open it in Excel*

You can process the csv file in exactly the same way as a text file. Use string handling commands to find the commas and the text between commas.

Exercises

1. Which of the flowcharts below represents a WHILE...ENDWHILE loop and which a REPEAT...UNTIL loop?   [1]

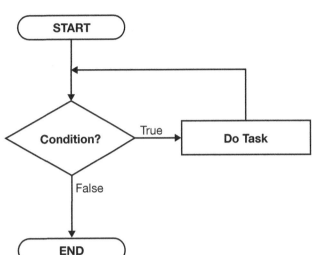

2. An integer 65 can be converted to a character using the statement:

        letter = CODE_TO_CHAR(65)

    The ASCII value corresponding to the letter "A" is the integer 65, so this statement would assign "A" to letter.

    (a) Write an algorithm which accepts three integers as input and outputs the corresponding letters as one word.   [4]

    (b) What word will be output if the user enters 66, 69 and 68?   [1]

3. An algorithm has been written to simulate a race. Each time the space bar is pressed, the position of the player moves up by 1. When the position reaches 100, the player has won.

    Here is the algorithm.

    ```
    constant PlayerKey = " "
    Position ← 0
    REPEAT
       KeyPressed ← USERINPUT
       IF KeyPressed = PlayerKey THEN
          Position ← Position + 1
       ENDIF
    UNTIL Position = 100
    ```

    (a) State what is meant by selection and iteration using examples from the algorithm.   [4]

    (b) To make the game more interesting, the rules are changed. Each time the spacebar is pressed, the position of the player will now move up by a random number between 1 and 4.

         State **two** changes that need to be made to include this new rule. Justify each change. [4]

4. Fred has written an algorithm to record temperature readings of a patient every hour for 6 hours and record the number of times the temperature is greater than 38, which is defined as an incidence of fever. His algorithm is shown below.

```
1.    constant feverTemp ← 39
2.    temp ← 0
3.    hour ← 0
4.    total ← 0
5.    fever ← 0
6.    WHILE hour < 6
7.       OUTPUT "Enter temperature: "
8.       temp ← USERINPUT
9.       IF temp > feverTemp THEN
10.          fever ← fever + 1
11.      ENDIF
12.      total ← total + temp
13.      hour ← hour + 1
14.   ENDWHILE
15.   average ← total / hour
16.   OUTPUT "Average temperature: ", average
17.   OUTPUT "Incidences of fever: ", fever
```

(a) State what is meant by a constant and give an example from the algorithm above. [2]

(b) State what is meant by a variable and give an example from the algorithm above. [2]

(c) Give an example of iteration in the pseudocode. [1]

(d) Show how the algorithm could be written using a **FOR...ENDFOR** loop instead of a **WHILE** loop. Which statements would need to be changed? [2]

(e) A validation routine is to be added to ensure that the user does not enter a temperature less than 35 or greater than 44. If they do, they are asked to re-enter the temperature.

Write statements to perform the validation, and indicate where the statements would be placed. [4]

5. (a) Write a program for a guessing game (using pseudocode or a flowchart) that does the following:

  - Assigns the word "cat" to a variable called `answer`

  - Assigns the user's input to a variable called `guess`

  - If the user correctly guesses "cat" then the program outputs "Correct", otherwise the program lets the user guess again

  - The game continues until the user guesses correctly [6]

(b) The programmer wants to improve the game.

State **two** simple changes that they could make to the game to improve it. [2]

6. The following algorithm uses two arrays to hold the marks scored by 5 pupils in two Computing exams. It should compare the marks achieved by each student in the two exams, and print out, for example:

James score improved by 3

David score dropped by 5

Some extra statements in the pseudocode algorithm will be needed in part (b) of the question.

Note that array indexing starts at 0.

```
name ← ["James", "David", "Isabella", "Sophie", "Ethan"]
score1 ← [65, 66, 72, 66, 81]
score2 ← [68, 61, 72, 69, 85]
totalScore1 ← 0
totalScore2 ← 0
totalPupil1 ← 0
totalPupil2 ← 0
FOR n ← 0 TO 4
   diff ← score2[n] - score1[n]
   IF diff ≥ 0 THEN
      OUTPUT name[n], "score improved by ", diff
   ELSE
      OUTPUT name[n], "score dropped by ", -diff
   ENDIF
ENDFOR
```

(a) Give an example in the pseudocode of:

   (i)   a statement which **initialises** a **variable** [1]

   (ii) an example of **definite iteration** [1]

   (iii) an example of a **selection** statement [1]

(b) What will be the **third** line output by the algorithm? [1]

(c) Complete the pseudocode to include the following two tasks:

   (i)   calculate and print the average mark obtained by each pupil over the two exams [4]

   (ii) calculate and print the average class score for each exam. [4]

Section 2B Programming techniques

Objectives

2B

- Understand the concept of subroutines
- Explain the advantages of using subroutines in programs
- Describe the use of parameters to pass data within programs
- Use subroutines that return values to the calling program
- Know that subroutines may declare their own variables, and that local variables:
  - only exist while the subroutine is executing
  - are only accessible within the subroutine
- Use local variables in subroutines and explain why it is good practice to do so
- Describe the structured approach to programming
- Explain the advantages of the structured approach
- Be able to write simple data validation and authentication routines
- Explain simple algorithms in terms of their inputs, processing and outputs
- Determine the purpose of simple algorithms
- Use trace tables to determine how simple algorithms work and what their purpose is
- Be able to select, use and justify suitable test data
- Explain the differences between low-level and high-level languages
- Understand the advantages and disadvantages of low-level and high-level languages
- List three common types of program translator: interpreter, compiler, assembler
- Explain the differences between the types of translator
- Explain when it would be appropriate to use each type of translator

2B.1 Procedures and functions

A **subroutine** is a named, self-contained section of code that performs a specific task. It may return one or more values but doesn't have to.

Imagine a recipe for a lemon meringue pie. You could have the recipe written out in one long list of instructions but it might be easier to separate out instructions for making pastry and making meringue, especially as these same instructions will be used in several other recipes as well.

The recipe for Lemon Meringue Pie might say:

1. Make short-crust pastry (see Recipe 5)

2. Make the meringue (see Recipe 12)

3. Mix the lemon rind, sugar etc.

Programs are similar. If you have some code that does a specific task, it can be written as a self-contained subroutine. It can then be used from anywhere in the program as needed, without writing all the instructions out again and again.

In a system that has several parts to it, perhaps selected from a menu, it is much easier to write and debug your code if it is written in subroutines. The main program might be an IF statement that calls subroutines to process each menu choice:

```
displayMenu
choice ← selectOption
IF choice = 1 THEN
   displayRules
ELSE
   playGame
ENDIF
```

In this example, a subroutine called `displayMenu` is first called to display a menu of options.

Then a second subroutine, `selectOption` is called which allows a user to select an option. The option selected is returned from the subroutine and assigned to a variable called choice.

Depending on the value of choice, either the subroutine `displayRules` or `playGame` is called.

You can see from this example that using subroutines makes the program structure really clear. Another benefit is that each subroutine can be written and tested in isolation from the other modules. This makes debugging much easier and, in the future, the program will be easier to maintain. Modules can also be reused in future programs

Subroutines

There are two different types of subroutine, called **procedures** and **functions**. We will look first at procedures.

Defining a procedure

This procedure prints a greeting.

```
SUBROUTINE greeting
   OUTPUT "Hello"
   OUTPUT "You're looking well"
ENDSUBROUTINE
```

To call this procedure, you write the name of the procedure wherever you want to call it.

```
greeting
```

Nothing is returned from a procedure – it just carries out the instructions and goes back to the next instruction after the call statement.

Receiving information through parameters

To make the subroutine more useful, you can pass it one or more **parameters**. The parameter is a variable named in the subroutine heading that will receive and use whatever value you pass it.

```
SUBROUTINE greeting(name)
    OUTPUT "Hello ", name
    OUTPUT "You're looking well"
ENDSUBROUTINE
```

To call this subroutine, you write the name of the subroutine wherever you want to call it, and specify what parameter is to be used.

```
greeting("James")
greeting("Helen")
OUTPUT "What is your name? "
firstname ← USERINPUT
greeting(firstname)
```

When this program is run, it will print

```
Hello James
You're looking well
Hello Helen
You're looking well
What is your name?
(user enters a name, e.g. Kerry)
Hello Kerry
You're looking well
```

You can pass as many parameters as you like, separated by commas.

> **Q1** Write a subroutine that accepts two parameters for oven temperature and number of eggs and prints out, for example, "Set the oven to 180 degrees. You will need 3 eggs."
> Write instructions to call the subroutine with two different sets of data.

Functions

Functions are similar to procedures; they are named, self-contained sections of code. The key difference is that they always return a value, using a RETURN statement.

We have already used several built-in functions such as CODE_TO_CHAR and CHAR_TO_CODE:

```
letter ← CODE_TO_CHAR(68)       # assigns "D" to letter
asciiValue ← CHAR_TO_CODE("B")  # assigns 66 to asciiValue
```

Example 1

Here is a sample function written in pseudocode to convert centimetres to inches:

```
SUBROUTINE cms2inches(metric)
   conversionFactor ← 2.54
   inches ← metric / conversionFactor
   RETURN inches
ENDSUBROUTINE
```

It could be used in a line of code like this:

```
OUTPUT "Enter your height in centimetres: "
heightMetric ← USERINPUT
OUTPUT "Your height in inches is ", cms2inches(heightMetric)
```

The subroutine in this case contains a RETURN statement, which identifies it as a function rather than a procedure.

> **Q2** Write a function to accept two numbers and return the maximum.

Local and global variables

A **global variable** is one which is declared (or in the case of Python, simply used) in the main program and is recognised in all the subroutines called from the main program.

Functions and procedures may use their own variables which are not known about or recognised outside the subroutine. In the function above which converts centimetres to inches, conversionFactor is a **local variable**, declared within the subroutine and only existing while the function is being executed. It is not recognised anywhere else in the program.

When a function or procedure is executed, it will automatically use the variables found locally, even if there is a global variable with the same name. If the variable is not found locally it will use the global variable. This means that the same variable identifiers can be used in several different procedures. This is useful if different people are writing different sections of the program.

Advantage of using local variables

- Using local variables in a subroutine is good practice because it keeps the subroutine self-contained. The subroutine can be used in any program and there will be no confusion over which variable names in the main program might conflict with names used in a subroutine.

- This also leads to the further advantage that the program will be easier to debug and maintain.

- If memory space is an issue, the use of local variables will save on memory as the space used by local variables is freed up when the subroutine completes.

Using local variables in a subroutine is a form of **abstraction**. The user of the subroutine needs only to know what **inputs** to the subroutine are required, and what the **output** will be. The detail of how the subroutine works and the variables it uses are hidden.

2B

The following function returns the average of three numbers n1, n2 and n3.

```
SUBROUTINE average(n1, n2, n3)
   total ← n1 + n2 + n3
   avg ← total/3
   RETURN avg
ENDSUBROUTINE
```

The function could be called using the statement

```
mean ← average(n1, n2, n3)
```

The return value, a local variable named `avg` in the subroutine, will be passed to `mean` in the calling routine.

The variable `total` is also a local variable inside the function `average`. If you try to print it outside the function, you will get an error message.

Example 2

Here is an outline program written in pseudocode, with global and local variables declared. This is not normally done in pseudocode but is done here in order to illustrate the scope of variables.

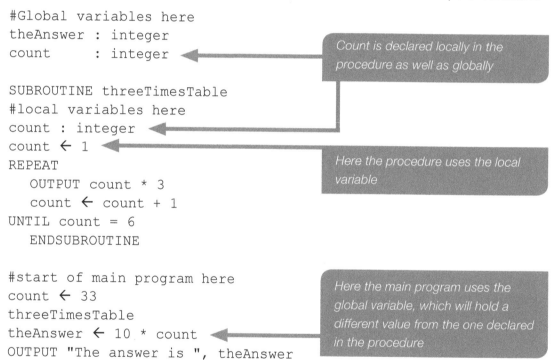

```
#Global variables here
theAnswer : integer
count     : integer
```
Count is declared locally in the procedure as well as globally

```
SUBROUTINE threeTimesTable
#local variables here
count : integer
count ← 1
REPEAT
   OUTPUT count * 3
   count ← count + 1
UNTIL count = 6
   ENDSUBROUTINE
```
Here the procedure uses the local variable

```
#start of main program here
count ← 33
threeTimesTable
theAnswer ← 10 * count
OUTPUT "The answer is ", theAnswer
```
Here the main program uses the global variable, which will hold a different value from the one declared in the procedure

This is the output screen for this algorithm/program.

```
3
6
9
12
15
The answer is 330
```

The program above is obviously daft but it illustrates the point.

Variables such as `count`, used to control loops, should always be local to that function or procedure. Even if you want to share data between subroutines, it is considered better practice to pass the data using parameters than to use global variables.

Local variables:

- only exist while the subroutine is executing
- are only accessible within the subroutine.

Study the algorithm below and answer the questions.

```
SUBROUTINE calcArea(radius)
    area ← pi * radius * radius
ENDSUBROUTINE
radius ← USERINPUT
pi ← 3.142
calcArea(radius)
OUTPUT "Area of the circle is ", area
```

(a) Give an example of a local variable and a global variable in this algorithm.

(b) What will be the first statement to be executed?

(c) Explain why the last line (the `OUTPUT` instruction) will produce an error.

(d) Correct the algorithm.

Advantages of using subroutines

Using subroutines to perform specific tasks in a program has many advantages.

- Breaking down or **decomposing** a large problem into sub-tasks, and writing each of these as a subroutine, makes the problem easier to solve
- Each subroutine can be **tested** separately
- Subroutines can be used several times within a program
- Subroutines can be stored in a **subroutine library** and used in different programs if needed
- Several programmers can work on a large program at the same time, writing different subroutines, so a large job will get done more quickly
- If the requirements of a problem change, it is much easier just to make a change in a subroutine than to search through a long program to find what lines need changing, so program **maintenance** is easier.

The structured programming approach

A structured programming approach is one which has the following characteristics:

- It uses a modularised approach. This means it uses subroutines to break down the program into manageable chunks of code. Each subroutine should have a clear, well documented interface (parameters and return value)
- It uses only the constructs of sequence, selection, iteration and recursion (recursion is not covered in this course).

Note that the term subroutine **interface** refers to the number, type and order of the parameters that appear in the subroutine header, and the type of the return value.

Advantages of the structured approach

The structured approach has all the advantages of using subroutines listed above. In addition, the use of just three or four programming structures makes a program relatively **easy to understand, debug and maintain**.

2B.2 Validation and authentication

Validating input data

Most programs require input from a user and so, in order to make sure the program will not crash or do something unexpected if the user enters something wrongly, all input data must be checked as soon as it is input. There are several types of **validation check** that can be carried out in a program:

- **Range check:** a number or date is within a sensible/allowed range
- **Type check:** data is the right type such as an integer, a letter or text
- **Length check:** text entered is not too long or too short – for example, a password is greater than 8 characters, a product description is no longer than 25 characters
- **Presence check:** checks that some data has been entered, i.e. that the field has not been left blank
- **Format check:** checks that the format of, for example, a postcode or email address is appropriate

Validation can only check if a data item is reasonable. It cannot tell if it is correct. This is an important difference. If a web form prompts for **Date of Birth**, the application can check that the data entered would be appropriate for that age group, but it cannot tell if you entered November instead of December by mistake.

Whilst validation ensures that the data entered are sensible, **verification** double-checks that it has been typed in correctly. Data is entered twice and the two versions are compared. If they are different the user can be prompted to try again. This is commonly used where email addresses and passwords are entered on forms.

Example 3

The following algorithm asks the user to enter their name, and performs a **length check**. The name must be between 2 and 20 characters.

```
OUTPUT "Please enter name: "
name ← USERINPUT "Please enter name: "
WHILE (LEN(name) < 2) OR (LEN(name) > 20)
   OUTPUT "Must be between 2 and 20 characters - please re-enter: "
   name ← USERINPUT
ENDWHILE
```

Example 4

The following algorithm asks the user to enter an integer between 17 and 30, and validates it by performing a range check. The number is then multiplied by 3 and the result printed out.

```
OUTPUT "Enter number between 17 and 30: "
num ← USERINPUT
WHILE num < 17 OR num > 30
    OUTPUT "Invalid number – please re-enter: "
    num ← USERINPUT
ENDWHILE
OUTPUT num * 3
```

Maintainability

There are several ways in which you can help to make your program code understandable.

- Use comments to say what the purpose of the program is, who wrote the program and when
- Use comments to explain how any difficult bit of code works, or what particular variables are used for
- Split the program into subroutines which each perform a single well-defined task
- Include comments with each subroutine to describe its purpose
- Use indentation so that it is clear where iteration and selection statements end. Some languages such as Python will give a syntax error if the indentation is not correct
- Use meaningful variable names for all variables
- Use constants for values such as VAT rate or π which will not change during execution of a program
- Aim for clarity rather than 'clever code' which is difficult for someone else to understand

All these techniques will help you when you return to a program after a few months and cannot remember what it is about or how it works.

Authentication routines

Authentication of an individual is used to make sure that a person is who they say they are. Biometric methods could include optical, facial or fingerprint recognition.

Other methods include asking the user to enter a user ID and password. A simple identification routine is used when you log into a school network, or an online shopping site. Usually, you will be assigned a user ID and you choose a password when you first log in. The password is encrypted and saved in a file. When you enter your user ID and password, the password is encrypted and compared to the one stored for that user ID.

Why are you normally only allowed three attempts to type in the correct password?

In Section 2A.3, Example 7 you saw a simple routine to check a user's password, giving them three attempts to get it right.

The next example shows a **verification** check, in which a new user logging on to a website for the first time chooses a password, and then has to re-enter it to make sure they typed in what they intended.

Select a Username:	
Please enter password:	
Confirm password:	
	Sign in

```
OUTPUT  "Please enter password: "
password ← USERINPUT
storedPassword ← password
OUTPUT "Confirm password: "
password ← USERINPUT
IF password = storedPassword THEN
   OUTPUT "Password accepted"
ELSE
   OUTPUT "This is a different password"
ENDIF
```

2B

Q5 Can you think of any other checks that should be made on a user password before it is accepted?

Amend the routine so that the user can start again if their password is rejected.

2B.3 Determining the purpose of algorithms

Several of the earlier examples of algorithms included a description of what function they are carrying out. One way of finding out what an algorithm does is to produce a **trace table**. This shows how the value of a variable changes as each step of the algorithm is executed.

In simple terms, an algorithm has one or more **inputs**, some **processing** steps, and **output**, which is the solution to the problem. In any algorithm, you should be able to identify where the inputs, processing and outputs are taking place

Example 5

Examine the following algorithm and identify

- an input statement

- the processing statements

- an output statement.

Produce a trace table for the algorithm. By inspecting how the variable values change, determine the purpose of the algorithm.

```
1. total ← 0
2. conversion ← 128
3. FOR count ← 1 TO 8
4.    digit ← USERINPUT
5.    value ← digit * conversion
6.    total ← total + value
7.    conversion ← conversion/2
8. ENDFOR
9. OUTPUT total
```

Input takes place at line 4.

Processing takes place between lines 3 and 8.

Output takes place at line 9.

The following digits are input: 1, 1, 0, 1, 1, 0, 1, 0

The trace table below has headings corresponding to each variable in the program. The order of the headings has been chosen so that count is at the beginning of the line, because it changes value before the other variables.

count	digit	value	total	conversion
			0	128
1	1	128	128	64
2	1	64	192	32
3	0	0	192	16
4	1	16	208	8
5	1	8	216	4
6	0	0	216	2
7	1	2	218	1
8	0	0	218	
		OUTPUT:	218	

The variable called `conversion` gives a strong clue as to what the purpose of the algorithm is.

We can see from this trace table that the algorithm is converting an 8-bit binary number into a base 10 (decimal) number.

Notice here the use of **meaningful variable names** which are a key part of understanding or interpreting the function of an algorithm.

Q6 Complete the trace table for the following algorithm and state its function.

```
total ← 0
FOR count ← 1 to 4
    base ← USERINPUT
    height ← USERINPUT
    value ← (base * height) * 0.5
    total ← total + value
ENDFOR
OUTPUT total / 4
```

Use the following input values: 10, 20, 8, 6, 16, 12, 15, 40

total	count	base	height	value	OUTPUT
0	1	10	20	100	

Sometimes you can figure out what the algorithm is doing without having a trace table. In the next question, you are not given the user input and you would not want to draw a trace table with 100 lines.

2B

Q7 Determine the purpose of the following algorithm.

```
t1ZeroOrMore ← 0
t2LessThanZero ← 0
totalTemp ← 0
FOR count ← 1 TO 100
    temperature ← USERINPUT
    IF temperature ≥ 0 THEN
        t1ZeroOrMore ← t1ZeroOrMore + 1
    ELSE
        t2LessThanZero ← t2LessThanZero + 1
    ENDIF
    totalTemp ← totalTemp + temperature
ENDFOR
meanTemperature ← totalTemp / 100
OUTPUT t1ZeroOrMore, t2LessThanZero
OUTPUT meanTemperature
```

Here is a more difficult question. Look for clues and think of algorithms that you have already studied. Can you remember an algorithm in which you swapped items in an array?

Q8 Study the following algorithm.

```
item ← [34, 26, 37, 12, 73, 11, 47]
n = LEN(item)
FOR i ← 0 TO n - 2
    FOR j ← 0 TO n - i - 2
        IF item[j] > item[j+1] THEN
            swap the items
        ENDIF
    ENDFOR
ENDFOR
```

(a)   Complete the pseudocode for "swap the items".

(b)   Use the headings given below for a trace table and fill in additional rows for i = 0 and j = 0 to 5.

(c)   State the purpose of the algorithm.

i	j	item[0]	item[1]	item[2]	item[3]	item[4]	Item[5]	Item[6]	n
		34	26	37	12	73	11	47	7
0	0								

2B.4 Errors and testing

When you write a program in a high-level programming language, a translator (compiler or interpreter, see Section 2B.5) will scan each line of code and convert it into machine code. As you will already have found out, programming is not as easy as it looks!

- Firstly, it is very easy to make mistakes typing in the code, for example typing "prnt" instead of "print". These are syntax errors.

- Secondly, once you have corrected all the syntax errors, the code may run but not do what you want. This means there are logic errors in your program.

Syntax errors

The translator expects commands to have a certain format, called syntax, just like a sentence in English has grammar rules. Syntax is a set of rules which defines the format of each command.

For example, in Visual Basic an IF statement must have this format:

```
If x = 10 Then
   grade = "Pass"
Else
   grade = "Fail"
End If
```

In Python, the format of an `IF` statement is written slightly differently:

```
if x == 10:
    grade = "Pass"
else
    grade = "Fail"
```

Q9 If you put `end if` at the end of the `if` statement in Python, you will see a message similar to the one below when you try to execute the code. How else does the syntax of the `if` statement in Python differ from that of Visual Basic?

```
line 18
end if
   ^
SyntaxError: invalid syntax
```

Without the correct key words the compiler will not be able to translate it into machine code and will give a syntax error.

Some common syntax errors include:

- mistyping a key word: `WRIET` instead of `WRITE`

- missing key words out of constructs such as starting a `REPEAT` loop but not writing `UNTIL` anywhere

- opening brackets but not closing them

- not having the right number of parameters inside brackets for functions, for example:
  `answer = RANDOM_INT(100)` will give a syntax error if the language expects another parameter to state the range:
  `answer = RANDOM_INT(1, 100)`

A program will not compile or run if there are syntax errors.

Logic errors

Once the code is written correctly, with no syntax errors, the program will compile. The program can then be run – but just because it will run, this does not mean that it is working correctly. Often when a program is run it doesn't do quite what is expected. This is called a **logic error**.

Typical logic errors that you have probably coded already include:

- Missing brackets from mathematical calculations:
  `NetPay = GrossPay - TaxFreePart * TaxRate`

  is not the same as:
  `NetPay = (GrossPay - TaxFreePart) * TaxRate`

- Loops that do not execute the correct number of times because a condition is written wrongly, e.g.
  `x > 10` instead of `x >= 10`

- variables that have not been initialised, or have been initialised in the wrong place (often incorrectly initialised inside the loop instead of just before it).

- flawed algorithms that just don't do what they were intended to do. Capturing all of the complexities of real-life scenarios in code is difficult and users always manage to do something to the input that you didn't cater for!

Often these logic errors are hard to spot. You should always do a visual check of output to check it isn't ridiculous but you also need to do some systematic testing to make sure the program really does behave as expected.

Q10 The flowchart below does not produce correct results.

Study it and state the likely purpose of the algorithm. Find the error(s) in the flowchart and produce a corrected version. Explain what the errors are in the original attempt.

```
                    START
                      |
                      v
              INPUT temp1,
                temp2
                      |
                      v
            diff ← temp1 - temp2
                      |
                      v
                 Is diff >        Yes
                   0?          ------->  diffPos ← diffPos + 1
                      |                       |
                   No |  <--------------------
                      v
            diffNeg ← diffNeg + 1
                      |
                      v
     Yes          Any
   <------        more?
                      |
                   No |
                      v
                 OUTPUT
                 diffPos
                 diffNeg
                      |
                      v
                    END
```

Testing

How do you know if your program really works? It may run and produce output but you need to check that the output is as expected. If you made a spreadsheet that multiplied pounds by a conversion rate to get dollars you would probably type in an easy number like £10 to see if the number of dollars looked right. We test programs in a similar way. We decide on some sensible test values to put into the program to test that the outputs are what we expect.

Planning how to test a program

A good way of planning your testing is to write down what sample data you will use to make sure the program works correctly, whatever the input. This is a **test plan**. It is important that you think about this before you write the program so you don't move the goalposts later. Remember, the aim of testing is to try and identify, for example, errors in calculations or user input which the program cannot handle, not to prove that the program usually works correctly.

You can formalise your plan by using a table with the following headings:

Test purpose	Test data	Expected outcome	Actual outcome

The first three columns are part of the design and planning stage and the final column is completed when you test the finished program.

If numbers or dates are being entered by the user then you should use test data that checks normal (typical), boundary (extreme) and erroneous data. **Boundary data** includes both ends of the allowed range as well as data that should not be allowed, just outside this range e.g.:

✘	✔	✔	✘
0	1	to	10	11

Allowed range of input values

The test plan for testing this validation could look like this:

Test purpose	Test data	Expected outcome
1 Check lowest valid number between 1 and 10	1 (lowest valid number)	Input is accepted
2 Check highest valid number between 1 and 10	10 (highest valid number)	Input is accepted
3 Check invalid boundary data outside lower limit	0 (not allowed)	Error message is displayed and user is asked to enter number again
4 Check invalid boundary data outside upper limit	11 (not allowed)	Error message is displayed and user is asked to enter number again
5 Check valid entry between 1 and 10	5 (typical number)	Input is accepted
6 Check invalid non-numeric entry	? (non-numeric entries not allowed)	Error message is displayed and user is asked to enter number again

If for example a password is being entered, check what happens when you enter a valid password, an invalid password, and an empty string.

Test purpose	Test data	Expected outcome
7 Check a correct password works	"frogs" (correct password)	User allowed to continue
8 Check that an error message is displayed when an incorrect password is entered	"cats" (incorrect password)	Error message is displayed and user is asked to enter password again
9 Check that an error message is displayed when an empty string is entered	"" (empty string)	Error message is displayed and user is asked to enter password again

Using a trace table to detect errors

A trace table is useful for tracing a logic error if a test does not give the expected result.

Example 6

The algorithm is designed to work out the average test scores for a class of 10 students. The scores have already been input into an array called "scores". The average should be the sum of the scores divided by the number of scores. Here is the algorithm:

```
count ← 0
totalScore ← 0
REPEAT
    totalScore ← totalScore + scores[count]
    count ← count + 1
UNTIL count = 9
OUTPUT totalScore / 10
```

Let's assume we have the following scores (out of 10) in the array:

Scores:

0	1	2	3	4	5	6	7	8	9
4	6	7	2	5	7	8	9	10	7

The total of these scores is 65. The average should be 65/10 = 6.5

The trace table for this algorithm looks like this:

scores[count]	totalScore	count	output
	0	0	
4	4	1	
6	10	2	
7	17	3	
2	19	4	
5	24	5	
7	31	6	
8	39	7	
9	48	8	
10	58	9	5.8

The total of these scores is 58, making the average 5.8.

The trace table shows that we exited the loop because count = 9, without processing the 10th result!

The algorithm needs adjusting so the loop says:

```
UNTIL count = 10 (or alternatively, UNTIL count > 9)
```

2B.5 Classification of programming languages

Programming languages can be broadly divided into two categories:

- **low-level languages** (processor-specific assembly languages and machine code)

- **high-level languages** such as Python, Visual Basic, Delphi, Java and many others

The program code, once translated into binary, is referred to as **machine code**. To write code at the processor level we use **assembly language**. There are lots of different assembly languages; one for each different processor architecture. The code is written using **mnemonics**, abbreviated text commands such as LDA (LOAD), STO (STORE), and ADD. Machine code is also processor-specific.

Human beings find it easier to write programs in languages that are suited to the type of problem they are trying to solve and that look more like normal languages, and **high-level languages** were invented for this. There are many different programming languages to suit different types of problem. For example, you might use Visual Basic to write a forms-based data processing application but you might use Java to code web-based applets.

Differences between high-level and low-level languages

Type of language	Example	Characteristics	Sample instructions

High-level language	Python, Visual Basic, Java, C++	Independent of hardware (portable)
		Translated using a compiler or interpreter
		One statement translates into many machine code instructions
			`rate = 3.02`
			`used = 5672`
			`billAmount = rate * used`

Low-level language	Assembly language	Translated using an assembler One statement translates into one machine code instruction	`LDA #34` `STO &39FC`
	Machine code	Executable binary code produced by compiler, interpreter or assembler	`1010100011010101` `0100100101010101`

High-level languages such as Python and Visual Basic have the following features, which are not available in low-level languages:

- Selection and iteration constructs such as IF...THEN...ELSE, FOR...ENDFOR, WHILE...ENDWHILE

- Boolean operators such as AND, OR and NOT which enable complex conditional statements to be written

- Identifiers using an unlimited number of alphabetic and numeric characters and some special characters means that variable names can be made meaningful, for example averageTemperature, eveningRate1

- Data structures such as arrays, as well as user-defined data types such as records.

Low-level languages have a much more limited number of programming constructs, with selection and iteration being performed using "compare and branch" instructions. These languages are harder to learn, more time-consuming to code and more difficult to debug.

Advantages and use of high-level languages

Most software is developed using a high-level language for the following reasons:

- High-level languages are relatively easy to learn and much faster to program in.

- Since statements written in these languages look a bit like English or maths, they are easier to read and understand, debug and maintain. Complex assignment statements such as

$$x = (sqrt(b^2 - 4 * a * c))/(2 * a)$$

  mean that a program in a high-level language is generally much closer to the algorithm for solving the problem, and therefore much more straightforward to code

- Specialised high-level languages have been developed to make the programming as quick and easy as possible for particular applications. SQL, for example, was specifically written to make it easy to search and maintain databases. HTML, CSS and JavaScript were developed to enable people to create web pages and websites.

Advantages and use of low-level languages

Assembly language is often used in **embedded systems** such as the computer systems that control a washing machine, automobile, traffic lights or a robot. It has the following features which make it suitable for this type of application:

- It gives the programmer complete control over the system components so it can be used to **control and manipulate specific hardware components**

- Very efficient code can be written for a particular type of processor, so it will occupy **less memory** and **execute faster** than a compiled high-level language

Differences between assembly code and machine code language

Machine code is the code executed by the processor, and consists only of 0s and 1s. Each type of processor has its own machine code instruction set, and all programs, whether written in a high-level language or in assembly language, have to be translated into machine code before they can be executed.

Translating programs into machine code

Translators are a type of system software (*see Section 4: Computer systems*). There are three types of translator program that do this:

Assembler

An **assembler** converts assembly language into machine code. This is a simple conversion as, in general, every assembly language instruction is translated into a single machine code instruction. Typically, each different type of processor uses a different assembly language and a different assembler.

However, for many architectures there is a wide choice of assemblers and some assemblers can assemble code for different processor architectures.

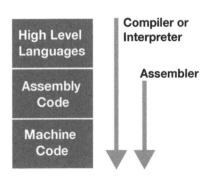

Compiler

A **compiler** translates a program written in a high-level programming language into machine code. This is a more complex translation as a single instruction can result in many machine code instructions. A program written and compiled on one type of computer would have to be compiled again to run on a computer with a different type of processor with a different set of machine code instructions.

The code written by the programmer is known as **source code**, and the machine code produced by the compiler is called object code. When you buy commercial software you are buying the **object code**, and you do not need the compiler in order to run the software.

For the developer, this has the advantage that someone buying the software cannot see the source code or copy it.

Interpreter

An **interpreter** is also used to translate high-level language code into machine code. An interpreter executes the program directly, translating each statement into a sequence of calls to one or more subroutines already compiled into machine code. You must have the interpreter installed on your computer in order to run the software.

A long, complex program will take considerably more time to execute if it is being interpreted. For example, if a loop is performed 10,000 times, the lines within the loop are translated 10,000 times.

The distinction between a compiler and an interpreter is not completely clear-cut, however. Some languages, such as **Java**, are compiled into an intermediate stage called **bytecode**. This can be interpreted and run on many different types of processor using an appropriate bytecode interpreter.

JavaScript, which is used in creating web pages, is interpreted; the source code is included in the web page and then interpreted in the browser.

The table below compares compilers and interpreters:

Compiler	Interpreter
Translates the whole program to produce the executable object code	Translates and executes one line at a time
Compiled program executes faster as it is already in machine code	Interpreted programs take more time to execute because each instruction is translated before it is executed
Customers do not need to have the compiler installed on their computer to run the software	Customers must have the interpreter installed on their computer and they can see the source code
Customers cannot see the actual source code when you distribute the program	Customers can see the source code and could copy it
Used for software that will be run frequently or copyright software sold to a third party	Used for program development and when program must be able to run on multiple hardware platforms

Exercises

1. (a) The following pseudocode uses a function which accepts a time in hours, minutes and seconds and converts this to a number of seconds.

    ```
    SUBROUTINE timeInSeconds(hours, minutes, seconds)
        timeElapsed ← (hours * 60 * 60) + (minutes * 60) + seconds
        RETURN timeElapsed
    ENDSUBROUTINE
    ```

    Write one or more pseudocode statements to call the function and
    print `timeElapsed` in seconds. [3]

    (b) Write a procedure which accepts a person's age as a parameter.
    If the age is less than 17, display:

    `You cannot hold a full driving licence`

    Otherwise, display:

    `You are eligible for a full driving licence`

    Show how you would call the procedure. [4]

2. (a) Explain what is meant by structured programming. [2]

    (b) Give **four** advantages of using structured programming techniques. [4]

3. The pseudocode below represents a function called `ArrayAverage`.

    `ArrayAverage` is used to find the average of all the numbers stored in an array.

    Note: line numbers have been shown but are not part of the function.

    ```
    1  SUBROUTINE ArrayAverage(numbers)
    2     total ← 0
    3     FOR i ← 0 TO LEN(numbers) - 1
    4        total ← total + numbers[i]
    5     ENDFOR
    6     RETURN total / LEN(numbers)
    7  ENDSUBROUTINE
    ```

    2B

    (a) How many parameters does the function `ArrayAverage` have? [1]

    (b) This function uses iteration. Give the line number on which iteration starts. [1]

    (c) This function uses variable assignment.
    Give the line number in the function where variable assignment is first used. [1]

    (d) Write one or more statements to call the function and output the average of the
    numbers in the array. [2]

4. The pseudocode below shows a function that is used to work out if a person is entitled to a discount in bus season ticket pricing, based on their age:

```
1.    SUBROUTINE discount(x)
2.      IF x > 65 THEN
3.        RETURN 1
4.      ELSE
5.        IF x < 16 THEN
6.          RETURN -1
7.        ELSE
8.          RETURN 0
9.        ENDIF
10.     ENDIF
11.   ENDSUBROUTINE
```

The subroutine `discount` returns an integer value.

(a) Explain why a Boolean return value could not have been used. [1]

(b) Each of the following expressions evaluates to an integer.
Give the integer value for each:

(i) `discount(78)` [1]

(ii) `discount(13)` [1]

(c) This function uses selection.

Give the line number on which selection starts. [1]

(d) The pseudocode above does not return the correct result for a 16 year old. They should get a discount if they are 16 or younger.

(i) What value does `discount(16)` currently return? [1]

(ii) What sort of error is this? [1]

(iii) Which line of code must be changed and what should it be changed to? [2]

5. A programmer is writing a revision app for a mobile phone.

(a) The program is written in a high-level code and then translated to machine code.
Describe **two** differences between high-level code and machine code. [4]

(b) One type of translator which can be used is an interpreter.

(i) Describe how an interpreter translates the high-level code to machine code. [2]

(ii) State the name of a different type of translator, other than an interpreter, which can be used to translate high-level code to machine code. [1]

6. (a) What is meant by a "robust" program? [2]

(b) Write an algorithm that asks a user to enter a number between 0 and 100. If the number is not in the range 0-100, a message "Out of range" is printed and they are asked to re-enter the value. [4]

Section 3 – Data representation

Objectives

3

- Understand the following number bases: decimal, binary, hexadecimal
- Convert between number bases
- Know that a bit is a fundamental unit of information, and a byte is a group of 8 bits
- Know the names and values of kB, MB, GB, TB
- Be able to perform binary arithmetic and binary shifts
- Describe the ASCII and Unicode character encoding systems and their purposes
- Describe how a bitmap represents an image using pixels and colour depth
- Calculate bitmap image file sizes based on the number of pixels and colour depth
- Convert binary data into a black and white image and vice versa
- Understand that sound must be converted to a digital form for storage in a computer
- Describe the digital representation of sound in terms of sampling rate and sample resolution
- Calculate sound file sizes
- Explain what data compression is
- Understand why data may be compressed and that there are different methods to compress data
- Explain how data can be compressed using Huffman coding
- Be able to interpret Huffman trees
- Be able to calculate the number of bits required to store compressed and uncompressed data
- Explain how data can be compressed using Run Length Encoding (RLE)

3.1 Storage units and binary numbers

Computers are made up of complicated hardware that stores and processes data. If you break a computer down into its most basic components you have millions of circuits that either allow electricity to flow, or not. Imagine a whole row of light switches that you can switch on and off in different combinations to mean different things. Each switch is either on or off. It has only two states, which can be represented by 1 or 0. This is called **binary**.

A single **1** or **0** is a **b**inary dig**it**, or a **bit** for short. A group of eight bits is called a **byte**. Imagine you've taken a small bite out of an apple, you might call that a nibble. So four bits, half a byte, is called a **nibble**.

Units

A byte is the smallest addressable unit of memory in a computer. Just as a kilometer is 1000 meters, we can group together 1000 bytes to make a **kilobyte**.

Memory size is measured in the following multiples:

Unit	Number of bytes	Equivalent decimal value	
Kilobyte (kB)	10^3	1,000	bytes
Megabyte (MB)	10^6	1,000,000	bytes
Gigabyte (GB)	10^9	1,000,000,000	bytes
Terabyte (TB)	10^{12}	1,000,000,000,000	bytes
Petabyte (PB)	10^{15}	1,000,000,000,000,000	bytes

(**NOTE:** 1GB = 1000kB etc. Internal memory often uses the kibibyte, where 1KiB (Kibibyte) = 2^{10} = 10,24 bytes, 1GiB (Gibibyte) = 2^{20} = 1,048,576 bytes, and so on).

Q1 (a) Convert 4,800MB into GB
(b) Convert 800TB into GB

Q2 (a) How big is a typical photograph file taken from a mobile phone camera?
(b) What is the average capacity of a hard disk or SSD on a computer?

Computers use the binary system to store numbers and perform binary arithmetic and logic operations. The storage capacities of computer system have grown, and the memory size of secondary storage systems is now commonly measured in terabytes (TB). Vast computers used in universities and industrial applications have memory storage which is now measured in petabytes. Scientists have estimated that the human brain has a memory capacity of 2.5 petabytes so computers seem to be catching up!

Binary to decimal conversion

Binary data uses only two digits, 0 and 1. Our decimal systems uses ten digits, 0 to 9. The number 75, for example, is 7 tens plus 5 units.

Imagine you are back in primary school, learning to add again. 7 + 5 = 12, so you write down the 2 units but carry the group of 10. 23 would be 2 groups of 10 and 3 units.

Counting in binary

Counting in binary is the same except instead of digits 0 to 9 we only have two digits, 0 and 1, so we carry the group of 2. This is known as base 2 or binary. This is how we count to ten in binary:

Decimal	Binary	
0	0	
1	1	
2	10	Notice that we now go to the second column – one group of 2, no units
3	11	One group of 2 plus one unit 2 + 1 = 3
4	100	Now we go to the third column, 2 groups of previous column, so this is 4
5	101	
6	110	
7	111	
8	1000	Every time we go to the next column it is two times the previous column
9	1001	
10	1010	

Can you see the pattern? The column headings in a binary number double each time:

$\times 2 \qquad \times 2 \qquad \times 2 \qquad \times 2 \qquad \times 2 \qquad \times 2 \qquad \times 2$

128	64	32	16	8	4	2	1
2x2x2x2x2x2x2	2x2x2x2x2x2	2x2x2x2x2	2x2x2x2	2x2x2	2x2	2	1
2^7	2^6	2^5	2^4	2^3	2^2	2^1	2^0

Q3 Looking at the table above, what is 2^8?

Storing larger numbers

In order to store larger numbers, computers group 2, 4, 8 or more bytes into units called **words**. On this course you will be dealing only with binary numbers held in a single 8-bit byte.

Decimal to binary conversion

To convert a decimal number to a binary number, use the column headings. You need to find the highest column heading that you can take away from the number and start there:

To convert the decimal number **57** into binary:

The highest column heading we can take out of 57 is 32 (the next one is 64, which is too high).

We can start by placing a "1" in the column headed 32 (57-32=25)

we can then place a "1" in the column headed 16 (25-16=9)

Finally place "1"s in columns 8 and 1 (9-8=1)

128	64	32	16	8	4	2	1
0	0	1	1	1	0	0	1

Here are some more examples:

Decimal	Binary							
	128	64	32	16	8	4	2	1
23 ⟶	0	0	0	1	0	1	1	1
84 ⟶	0	1	0	1	0	1	0	0
255 ⟶	1	1	1	1	1	1	1	1

You will notice in the examples above that we always write the binary numbers using eight bits. This is common practice. It is not incorrect to write the first binary value as 1 0 1 1 1 rather than 0 0 0 1 0 1 1 1 (without the leading zeros) but the second example is more commonly used as values are often stored in bytes.

> **Q4** Convert the following decimal numbers into binary.
>
> (a) 19
>
> (b) 63
>
> (c) 142

Binary to decimal conversion

To convert a binary number into decimal, add up the column values where a "1" appears. For example, to convert the binary number 01101100 to decimal, write each number under a column heading, starting on the right with the least significant digit:

128	64	32	16	8	4	2	1
0	1	1	0	1	1	0	0

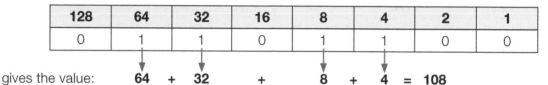

gives the value: **64** + **32**   +   **8** + **4** = **108**

More examples:

Decimal	Binary							
	128	64	32	16	8	4	2	1
126 ⟵	0	1	1	1	1	1	1	0
213 ⟵	1	1	0	1	0	1	0	1
255 ⟵	1	1	1	1	1	1	1	1

> **Q5** Convert the following binary numbers into decimal.
>
> (a) 00010111
>
> (b) 10010110
>
> (c) 11111111

3.2 Binary arithmetic and hexadecimal

Addition of binary numbers

Adding binary works in exactly the same way as adding decimal numbers except this time you carry groups of 2 instead of groups of 10:

Adding in decimal	Adding in binary
7 8 2 3 5 $\quad_1$ 9$_1$ 7 + ——————— 7 8 3 3 2 *Notice that you carry 1 when you get to 10 in a column so when 5+7=12, write 2 in that column but carry one group of ten.*	1 0 0 1 1 $\quad_1$ 1$_1$ 1$_1$ 1 + ——————— 1 1 0 1 0 *Notice that you carry 1 when you get to 2 in a column, so 1+1=2, write 0 in that column but carry one group of two.* *In the second column, 1+1+1=3, write a 1 in that column and carry one group of two to the third column.*

Adding three binary numbers

To add three binary numbers, add the first two, and then add the third to the result. For example, to add the three binary numbers 00101100, 00010001 and 10000101:

```
00101100        ┌ - - - ►00111101
00010001+       │         10000101+
—————————       │        —————————
00111101 - - - - ┘        11000010
```

> **Q6** Carry out the following binary number additions:
> (a) 00110011 + 01000110
> (b) 00010110 + 01110110
> (c) 00001111 + 01110011
> (d) 00101010 + 01111011
> (e) 00011100 + 01110011 + 01001101

Overflow

The biggest number you can represent with 8 bits is 255 (i.e. 128+64+32+16+8+4+2+1).

If you add two binary numbers together that result in a number bigger than 255, it will need 9 bits. A computer stores things in memory in a finite amount of space. If you cannot represent the number in that amount of space because it is too big, then **overflow** occurs.

For example:

```
(252)  11111100
(15)   00001111+
       —————————
(267) 100001011
```

The computer would need 9 bits to represent 267 so this 9th bit doesn't fit in the byte allocated. This is what is meant by an **overflow** error.

Binary shifts

If a binary number is shifted to the left this is equivalent to multiplying the number by 2 for each shift to the left.

For example: If we shift:

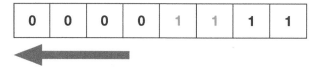

TWO places to the left we get the binary number:

(NOTE: we fill empty binary positions with 0s as we shift to the left)

The original binary number has a value of 15 (i.e. 8+4+2+1 = 15); the number after shifting two places to the left has the value 60 (i.e. 32+16+8+4 = 60). It is multiplied by 4, or 2^2.

Shifting binary numbers to the right has the opposite effect i.e. each shift to the right has the effect of dividing by 2. Thus if we shift:

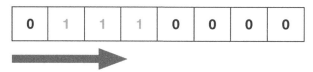

THREE places to the right we get the binary number:

The original binary value was 112 (i.e. 64 + 32 + 16 = 112) and the value after shifting three places to the right is 14 (i.e. 8 + 4 + 2 = 14). The number was divided by 8, and becomes 2^3. (NOTE: we fill empty binary positions with 0s as we shift to the right)

Multiplication/division by powers of 2

This gives an easy way to multiply and divide binary numbers by powers of 2, but can come at the expense of accuracy. For example 00000110 shifted right twice to divide by 4 would be 00000001. This is the equivalent of decimal 1, but 6 / 4 = 1.5.

- Shifting right one place divides the number by 2
- Shifting left one place multiplies the number by 2

This is equivalent to shifting a decimal number right or left – for example shifting 12300 right gives 1230, i.e. it divides the number by 10. Shifting left multiplies a decimal number by 10.

| Q7 | Write down the results after the following shift operations and write down the decimal values before and after the shifts:
(a) The number 11001100 is shifted TWO places to the right
(b) The number 00011001 is shifted TWO places to the left
(c) The number 11001000 is shifted THREE places to the right
(d) The number 00000111 is shifted FOUR places to the left
(e) The number 10000000 is shifted FIVE places to the right |

Hexadecimal number system

Which of these is easier to remember: **01011011** or **5B**? Humans are not very good at remembering long strings of numbers so, to make it easier, we can represent every group of 4 bits (known as a **nibble**) with a single digit.

The smallest value you can hold in 4 bits is 0000. The largest value is 1111. This means that we need to represent the decimal values 0 to 15 with a single digit. The trouble is, we only have numerical digits 0 to 9, so to get around this problem we use letters to represent the numbers 10, 11, 12, 13, 14 and 15.

This is called base 16 or, more commonly, **hexadecimal**. It is often abbreviated to **hex**.

Decimal	Binary	Hex
0	0000	0
1	0001	1
2	0010	2
3	0011	3
4	0010	4
5	0101	5
6	0110	6
7	0111	7
8	1000	8
9	1001	9
10	1010	A
11	1011	B
12	1100	C
13	1101	D
14	1110	E
15	1111	F
16	0001 1111	10
25555	1111 1111	FF

A single hex digit replaces 4 bits

15 is the biggest number you can have with 4 bits so 16 is one group of 16 and no units (just like we did before with binary)

255 is 15 groups of 16 + 15 units i.e. (15 x 16) + 15 = 240 + 15

Converting a binary number to hexadecimal

In GCSE Computing you will only need to work with 8-bit binary numbers, which can be represented as two hex digits. The left-hand hex digit represents groups of 16, the right-hand hex digit represents the units. For example, to convert the binary number 01011100 to hex:

The denary number 92 =   0101   1100   = 5C in hex
                            5   12   *(12 is replaced by C – see table above)*

Q8 Convert the following numbers from binary to hex:

(a) 00010111

(b) 11111100

(c) 00110010

(d) 11011100

Converting a decimal number to hexadecimal

To convert the decimal number 182 into hex the first step is to work out how many groups of 16 there are in 182. Secondly work out how many units are left over.

182 / 16 = 11 remainder 6

11 is B in hex. 6 is just 6 so 182 decimal = B6 hex

Alternatively, you can convert the decimal to binary first and then convert the binary to hex, as above.

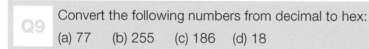

Q9 Convert the following numbers from decimal to hex:

(a) 77　　(b) 255　　(c) 186　　(d) 18

Converting hexadecimal to binary

Converting a hexadecimal number into binary is a simple matter of converting each hex digit into a group of 4 binary digits. For example, to convert the hex number **A7** to binary:

A　　**7**　　　　　　**A7**
↓　　　↓　　　　　　　↓
1 0 1 0　0 1 1 1　=　**1 0 1 0 0 1 1 1**

Further examples:　　**B 5**　is　1 0 1 1　　0 1 0 1
　　　　　　　　　　　F A　is　1 1 1 1　　1 0 1 0

Q10 Convert the following hexadecimal numbers into binary

(a) E4　　(b) 8A　　(c) FF　　(d) C1

Converting hexadecimal to decimal

To convert a hexadecimal number into decimal, multiply the heading or place values by the hex digit. For example, to convert the hex number **A7** to decimal:

A　　　　**7**　　　　　(remember column place values are: **16** and **1**)
↓　　　　　↓
(10 x 16)　+　(7 x 1)　=　**167**　(remember: A = 10)

Further examples:　　**7 F**　is　112 + 5　=　**1 2 7**
　　　　　　　　　　　C D　is　192 + 13　=　**2 0 5**

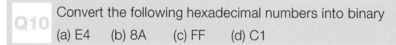

Q11 Convert the following hexadecimal numbers into decimal

(a) 77　　b) AF　　(c) 17　　(d) 20

Uses of hexadecimal

Hex numbers are expressed more compactly than binary numbers, and are much easier to understand and remember.

For this reason, hexadecimal numbers are often used instead of binary numbers and have several applications in computing.

One application you are probably familiar with is picking colours for a graphic.

Hex numbers are also used in assembly language instructions such as ADD &4F3A.

3.3 ASCII and Unicode

Every time a character is typed on a keyboard a code number is transmitted to the computer. The code numbers are stored in binary. PCs sometimes use a **character set** called **ASCII**, American Standard Code for Information Interchange.

The table below shows a version of ASCII that uses 7 bits to code each character. The biggest number that can be held in seven bits is 1111111 in binary (127 in decimal). Therefore 128 different characters can be represented in the ASCII character set (using codes 0 to 127).

7-bit ASCII Table

ASCII	Dec	Binary	ASCII	Dec	Binary	ASCII	Dec	Binary	ASCII	Dec	Binary
NULL	000	000 0000	space	032	010 0000	@	064	100 0000	`	096	110 0000
SOH	001	000 0001	!	033	010 0001	A	065	100 0001	a	097	110 0001
STX	002	000 0010	"	034	010 0010	B	066	100 0010	b	098	110 0010
ETX	003	000 0011	#	035	010 0011	C	067	100 0011	c	099	110 0011
EOT	004	000 0100	$	036	010 0100	D	068	100 0100	d	100	110 0100
ENQ	005	000 0101	%	037	010 0101	E	069	100 0101	e	101	110 0101
ACK	006	000 0110	&	038	010 0110	F	070	100 0110	f	102	110 0110
BEL	007	000 0111	'	039	010 0111	G	071	100 0111	g	103	110 0111
BS	008	000 1000	(	040	010 1000	H	072	100 1000	h	104	110 1000
HT	009	000 1001	)	041	010 1001	I	073	100 1001	i	105	110 1001
LF	010	000 1010	*	042	010 1010	J	074	100 1010	j	106	110 1010
VT	011	000 1011	+	043	010 1011	K	075	100 1011	k	107	110 1011
FF	012	000 1100	,	044	010 1100	L	076	100 1100	l	108	110 1100
CR	013	000 1101	–	045	010 1101	M	077	100 1101	m	109	110 1101
SO	014	000 1110	.	046	010 1110	N	078	100 1110	n	110	110 1110
SI	015	000 1111	/	047	010 1111	O	079	100 1111	o	111	110 1111
DLE	016	001 0000	0	048	011 0000	P	080	101 0000	p	112	111 0000
DC1	017	001 0001	1	049	011 0001	Q	081	101 0001	q	113	111 0001
DC2	018	001 0010	2	050	011 0010	R	082	101 0010	r	114	111 0010
DC3	019	001 0011	3	051	011 0011	S	083	101 0011	s	115	111 0011
DC4	020	001 0100	4	052	011 0100	T	084	101 0100	t	116	111 0100
NAK	021	001 0101	5	053	011 0101	U	085	101 0101	u	117	111 0101
SYN	022	001 0110	6	054	011 0110	V	086	101 0110	v	118	111 0110
ETB	023	001 0111	7	055	011 0111	W	087	101 0111	w	119	111 0111
CAN	024	001 1000	8	056	011 1000	X	088	101 1000	x	120	111 1000
EM	025	001 1001	9	057	011 1001	Y	089	101 1001	y	121	111 1001
SUB	026	001 1010	:	058	011 1010	Z	090	101 1010	z	122	111 1010
ESC	027	001 1011	;	059	011 1011	[	091	101 1011	{	123	111 1011
FS	028	001 1100	<	060	011 1100	\	092	101 1100	|	124	111 1100
GS	029	001 1101	=	061	011 1101	]	093	101 1101	}	125	111 1101
RS	030	001 1110	>	062	011 1110	^	094	101 1110	~	126	111 1110
US	031	001 1111	?	063	011 1111	_	095	101 1111	DEL	127	111 1111

Using the ASCII table in programming

The character codes are grouped and run in sequence; i.e. if 'A' is 65 then 'C' must be 67. The pattern applies to other groupings such as digits and lowercase letters, so you can say that since '7' is 55, '9' must be 57. Also, '7' < '9' and 'a' > 'A'.

Notice that the ASCII code value for '5' (0011 0101) is different from the pure binary value for 5 (0000 0101). That's why you can't calculate with numbers which are input as strings.

Character sets

Extended ASCII code

The basic ASCII codes use 7 bits for each character (as shown in the table above). This gives a total of 128 (2^7) possible unique symbols. The **extended ASCII** character set uses 8 bits, which gives an additional 128 characters (i.e. 256 in total). The extra characters represent characters from foreign languages and special symbols such as é, € or ←.

Unicode

Unicode is the new standard for representing the characters of all the languages of the world, including Chinese, Arabic, Japanese and Greek characters:

$$ \text{العربيّة}, \text{汉语}, \text{תִירְבַע}, \text{ελληνικά} $$

Unicode uses between 8 and 32 bits per character and has the advantage that it can represent many more unique characters than ASCII because of the larger number of bits available to store a character code. It uses the same codes as ASCII up to 127.

Its major advantage is that it provides a unique standard for all the world's writing systems. It allows for multilingual text in any language.

> **Q12** Using extended 8-bit ASCII, how many bytes would be required to store the phrase 'Computer Science'?

3.4 Images

Images can be stored in different ways on a computer. A drawing that you create in PowerPoint is a **vector** graphic. It is made up of lines and shapes with specific properties such as line style, line colour, fill colour, start point and end point. The computer stores all of this data about each shape in binary.

When you take a photograph on a digital camera, the image is not made up of individual shapes. The picture somehow has to capture the continuously changing set of colours and shades that make up the real-life view. To store this type of image on a computer the image is broken down into its smallest elements called **pixels**. A pixel (short for picture element) is a single point in an image, which can have its colour set independently. The whole image may be set to, for example, 600 pixels wide by 400 pixels high.

The **size** of an image is expressed directly as the width in pixels by height in pixels, e.g. 600 x 400.

10	10	10	10	10	10	10	10
10	00	10	00	10	00	10	10
10	10	00	00	00	10	10	10
10	00	00	01	00	00	10	10
10	10	00	00	00	00	10	10
10	00	10	00	11	00	10	10
10	10	10	10	11	10	10	10
10	10	10	10	10	11	10	10
10	11	11	11	10	11	11	10
10	10	11	11	11	11	10	10
10	10	10	10	11	10	10	10

If the size of a picture is increased, then more pixels will need to be stored. This increases the size of the image file. This is a **bitmap** image.

Making an image file

This image of a flower uses 4 colours. Therefore 2 bits are needed to record the colour of each pixel as 11, 10, 01, 00:

11	10	01	00

The number of bits used to store each pixel dictates how many colours an image can contain. 8 bits per pixel will give 256 possible colours.

Colour depth

The number of bits per pixel is referred to as the **colour depth**. To work out the minimum required colour depth from the number of colours in the image, convert the number of colours to a power of 2.

For up to:

$2 = 2^1$ colours	1 bit is required
$4 = 2^2$ colours	2 bits are required
$8 = 2^3$ colours	3 bits are required
...	
$256 = 2^8$ colours	8 bits are required
...	
$65,536 = 2^{16}$ colours	16 bits are required

If the **colour depth** is increased, more bits are used to represent each pixel, and the overall size of the file will increase.

If we record the value of each pixel in the flower image, starting from the top left-hand corner and going left to right across each row, we end up with the following data file:

```
10 10 10 10 10 10 10 10
10 00 10 00 10 00 10 10
10 10 00 00 00 10 10 10
10 00 00 01 00 00 10 10
etc.
```

Q13 Convert the following binary data into a 5 x 5 pixel image, where 1 represents black and 0 represents white: 1 1 1 1 1 0 0 1 0 0 0 0 1 0 0 0 0 1 0 0 0 0 1 0 0

Q14 Convert the black and white image below into binary data, where 1 represents black and 0 represents white.

The effect of colour depth and image size

Colour depth is used to describe the number of bits used to represent each pixel. The higher the number of colours, the more faithful the image will be. This also affects the file size of the image.

We can have monochrome (black and white), grey scale (usually 256 shades of grey), 16-bit colour and 32-bit colour (known as true colour), for example.

2 colours   *4 colours*   *8 colours*   *16 colours*   *256 colours*   *65,536 colours*   *16.7m colours*

If the file size of the first image, with a bit-depth of 1 and only two colours, is 60kB, the second will be 120kB, the third 180kB. The final image, with 24-bit colour depth, will be 24 x 60kB = 1,440kB.

The **size** of an image is the number of pixels (picture elements) or dots that make up an image. The greater the number of pixels per inch, the sharper the image will be, and the larger the file size of the image. Pixel density, measured in pixels per inch (PPI) is used to describe the resolution of a computer screen, camera or scanner.

An image from the Internet is typically 72PPI, which is a low resolution. If you try to enlarge the image on the screen, the software makes up for the pixels which don't exist and you get a blurred image. The small icon image shown below becomes blurred if you increase its size on screen.

Calculating the file size

The file size depends on the colour depth and the number of pixels in the image.

Size in bits = image width x image height x colour depth
Size in bytes = (image width x image height x colour depth) / 8

Example 1

An image captured in 256 colours, with a size of 2,100 pixels by 1,500 pixels, is saved on a memory stick. What is the size in bytes of the file?

Size in bytes = (width x height x colour depth) / 8 bits

= (2,100 x 1,500 x 8) / 8

= 3,150,000 bytes (3.15MB)

> **Q15** Calculate the size in bytes of a black and white image that is 96 pixels wide and 1,024 pixels high.

3.5 Sound

Sound waves are **analogue**, which means continuously changing. Anything stored on a computer has to be stored in a **digital** format as a series of binary numbers. To store sound on a computer we need to convert the waveform into a numerical representation. The device that takes real-world analogue signals and converts them to a digital representation is called an **Analogue-to-Digital Converter (ADC)**.

For sound waves, the analogue signal is converted as follows:

1. Analogue sound is received by a microphone
2. This is converted into an electrical analogue signal
3. The signal amplitude (height of the wave) is measured at regular intervals (**sampled**)
4. The values are rounded to a level (quantisation)
5. The values are stored as a series of binary numbers.

A **sample** is a measure of amplitude at a point in time. The accuracy with which an analogue sound wave is converted to a digital format depends on two things, **sample resolution** and **sample rate**.

The **sample resolution** is the number of bits used to store each sample. The two graphs below show how the amplitude of a wave is less accurately represented with a 2-bit sample resolution than with a 4-bit sample resolution.

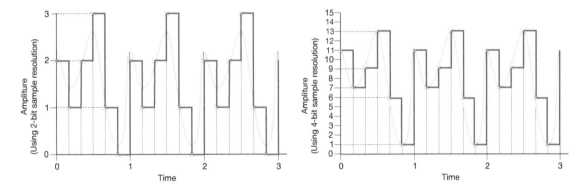

Graphs showing the effect on recording accuracy with changes in sample resolution

The **sample rate** is the frequency with which you record the amplitude of the sound, i.e. the number of samples per second. This is usually measured in Hertz, where 1 Hertz = 1 sample per second. The more frequently the sound is sampled, the better the quality and smoother the playback will sound. The two graphs below show how changing the sample rate increases or decreases the accuracy of the digital representation.

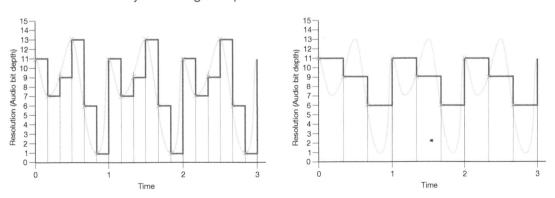

Graphs showing the effect on recording accuracy with changes in sample rate

Example 2 Calculating the size of a sound file

The file size of a sample = sample rate x sample resolution x number of seconds

A sample rate of 44.1kHz is typically used for CD audio, with a sample resolution of 16 bits per sample.

The file size of a sample lasting 5 seconds would be:

$$(44.1 \times 1000 \times 16 \times 5) / 8 \text{ bytes}$$

$$= (44.1 \times 16 \times 5) / 8 \text{ kB}$$

$$= 441\text{kB}$$

> **Q16** Calculate the file size in bytes of a 10 second radio jingle, using a sample rate of 8,000Hz and a 16 bit sample resolution.

3.6 Compression

When data is transmitted across the Internet it will go through many different physical links between routers. The connection from a computer or a LAN into the Internet is likely to be the slowest part of this route, as you probably know from experience. At home you may have quite a slow network connection and it may take a while for web pages to load.

One way of speeding up the rate at which files can be transmitted across the Internet is to compress them to make them smaller. Smaller files take less time to transmit over a network.

Understanding how compression affects files is important as the type of compression selected will affect how the image looks or the audio track sounds. The final use of the file will dictate how much you can compress the files and still have a file that is useable.

To summarise, compression is used in order to:

- reduce the amount of storage needed on a computer to save files

- allow large files to be transmitted as an email attachment; many email servers limit the size of a file that can be sent and compression can reduce the file size to allow users to send it

- allow a file to be transmitted in less time, owing to the smaller file size.

Lossy compression

Lossy compression: a data encoding method where files are compressed by removing some of the detail. For example, photographs can be stored using fewer colours so fewer bits are needed per pixel. This type of compression is used to compress images, audio files and video files.

Here is a photograph so you can see the difference:

JPEG version

GIF version

Lossless compression

This is a data encoding method where files are compressed but no data is lost – an essential factor for text and data files. For example, bank records must keep all of the data; you cannot transmit a bank statement and miss out a few zeros because they don't matter too much!

It could be used to compress data files, for example by "zipping" them using a utility program such as WinZip, before attaching them to an email.

The following table shows different file types and file extensions used for different file formats.

Type	File suffix	Compression Type	Explanation
Bitmap	.bmp	-	Uncompressed still image file
JPEG	.jpg	Lossy	Good for photographs. Colour depth = 24 bits, RGB, 16.7 million different colours
Graphic Interchange Format	.gif	Lossless	Colour depth = 8 bits (only 256 colours) Good for images with large areas of solid colour Ideal for web graphics
MP3	.mp3	Lossy	Audio files: Designed for downloading music from the Internet. In MP3 format you could fit 120 songs on a CD.

Run length encoding

Run length encoding (RLE) is a simple form of lossless data compression in which runs of data (sequences of data all having the same value) are stored using frequency/data pairs. For example, the black and white image below in uncompressed form would occupy 64 bits, with 1 representing white and 0 representing black.

It could be represented as:
11111111 10111111 00000011 00000011 00000000 00000000 00000000 10011001.

Using RLE, the first row of pixels could be represented as 8 1, meaning that there are 8 pixels each having a value of 1. The second row can be represented as 1 1 1 0 6 1 representing 1 white pixel, 1 black pixel and then 6 white pixels.

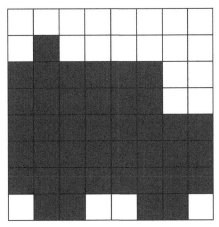

RLE is not so useful with files that don't have many runs, and can in fact increase the file size. It is most useful on simple images such as icons that contain many pixels that are the same colour.

Q17 Using RLE, show how the image below would be coded, if black is encoded as 0 and white as 1.

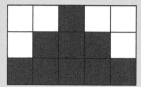

Huffman coding

Huffman coding is a compression technique used to reduce the number of bits used to represent each letter. The more frequently a letter appears in the text, the fewer bits are used to represent it in a text file.

Example 3

Consider the sentence PIPPA ATE A PEPPER. A table showing the frequency of each character, including spaces is created as the first step in building the Huffman tree. For example, there is one "I", one "R", and six "P"s in the sentence.

Character	I	R	T	A	E	SPACE	P
Frequency	1	1	1	3	3	3	6

You will only be required to interpret the tree, not build it. A Huffman tree for this sentence is shown below. It is a binary tree in which characters that occur most frequently are nearer the top and therefore require fewer characters to encode them, as described below.

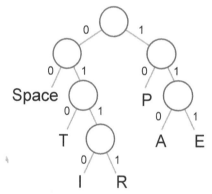

Using this Huffman tree, the coding for each character is derived from the path taken from the root node to the character. Branching left at a node is coded as 0, branching right is coded as 1.

Thus the character 'A' would be represented by the bit pattern 110 because from the top of the tree, you go right, right, left to reach 'A'. The encoding for 'T' would be 010 and for 'E', 111.

The total number of bits needed to represent the word "ATE" would be 3 + 3 + 3 = 9. In 7-bit ASCII, the number of bits required would be 3 x 7 = 21, representing a saving of 12 bits in the compressed format, with a 57% reduction in size.

Q18
(a) What would be the coding for the letters P, I, T?

(b) How many bits would these three letters take using the Huffman code?

(c) The sentence PIPPA ATE A PEPPER is represented in a total of 47 bits.
How many bits would be required to represent the sentence in ASCII?

(d) How many bits are saved by compressing PIT using Huffman coding?

Exercises

1. (a) Add the following two 8-bit binary numbers:

    0 0 1 1 0 1 0 1

    1 0 0 1 1 1 0 1   [2]

    (b) Add the following three 8-bit numbers:

    0 0 1 1 1 0 0 0

    1 0 0 0 1 0 1 1

    0 0 1 1 1 0 0 1   [2]

2. (a) The number 73 could be a decimal number or a hex number.

    (i) If 73 is a hex number, calculate its value as a decimal number.

    You **must** show your working.   [2]

    (ii) If 73 is a decimal number, calculate its value as a hex number.

    You **must** show your working.   [2]

    (b) Explain why people sometimes use hex numbers to represent numbers stored in computers, even though computers do not use hex numbers.   [3]

3. (a) Explain why data is stored in computers in a binary format.   [2]

    (b) In the ASCII character set, the character codes for three capital letters are given below.

Letter	ASCII character code
A	65
N	78
R	82

    (i) Explain how the ASCII character set is used to represent text in a computer.   [2]

    (ii) Convert the word RAN into binary using the ASCII character set.   [4]

    (iii) Name an alternative coding system which can represent characters in the alphabet of any language.   [1]

4. When recording a sound file on a computer, the sound needs to be sampled.

    (a) Describe how sampling is used when storing sound.   [2]

    (b) Explain the effect of the sampling rate on the size and quality of the sound file recorded. [3]

5. Files are often compressed before they are sent over the Internet.

    (a) State what is meant by compression.   [1]

    (b) State **two** advantages of compressing files before sending them over the internet.   [2]

6. Run length encoding (RLE) is a compression method.

   (a) Show how the first row of the following image would be represented without using compression, with white represented by 1 and black by 0. [1]

   (b) Show how the first line of the image would be represented using RLE [2]

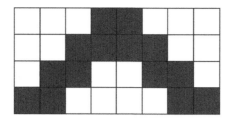

7. One method that can be used to compress text data is Huffman coding. To produce a Huffman code each character in a piece of text is placed in a tree, with its position in the tree determined by how often the character appears in the text.

   A Huffman tree of the text HELEN FEEDS THE EELS is shown below.

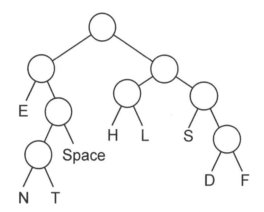

   Using this Huffman tree the coding for character H would be the bit pattern 100 because from the top of the tree, H is to the right, then to the left and then left again.
   The encoding for E would be 00.

   (a) Complete the table showing the Huffman coding for S, T and space. [3]

Character	Huffman coding
S	
T	
Space	

   (b) Using Huffman code the sentence HELEN FEEDS THE EELS can be stored in 57 bits. Calculate the number of bits that would be needed to store the sentence in ASCII. [3]

3

Section 4 – Computer systems

Objectives

- Construct truth tables for AND, OR and NOT gates
- Construct truth tables for simple logic circuits
- Interpret the results of truth tables
- Create, modify and interpret simple logic circuit diagrams
- Define the terms hardware and software and understand the relationship between them
- Explain what is meant by system software and application software and give examples of each
- Understand the need for, and functions of operating systems and utility programs
- Understand that the operating system handles management of the processor, memory, I/O devices, applications and security
- Explain the Von Neumann architecture
- Explain the role and operation of main memory, the ALU, control unit, clock and bus
- Explain the effects of clock speed, number of cores, cache size and cache type on CPU performance
- Understand and explain the Fetch-Execute cycle
- Understand the difference between main memory and secondary storage
- Understand the differences between RAM and ROM
- Understand why secondary storage is required
- Explain the operation of solid state, optical and magnetic storage
- Explain the advantages and disadvantages of solid state, optical and magnetic storage
- Explain the term 'cloud storage'
- Explain the advantages and disadvantages of cloud storage when compared to local storage
- Understand the term 'embedded system' and explain how it differs from a non-embedded system

4

4.1 Boolean logic

Binary logic in programming

Understanding how binary logic works will help your programming. In your programs you often use complex Boolean expressions to control loops and selection statements – for example:

```
WHILE NOT(EndOfFile) AND NOT (ItemFound)……

IF (X ≤ 10) OR (CurrentCharNum > LengthOfString) THEN ……
```

You have probably programmed a repeat loop to carry on until the user typed an "N" or "n". The loop would look something like this with the condition at the end:

```
REPEAT
   ¦
   ¦
   ¦
UNTIL (response = 'N')   OR   (response = 'n')
```
Boolean Expression   *Boolean Expression*

Each **Boolean expression** can be replaced with a letter which is called a **Boolean variable**.

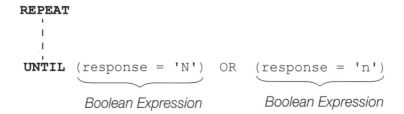

```
UNTIL (response = 'N')   OR   (response = 'n')
```
Replace with the   **Replace with the**
Boolean variable, X   **Boolean variable, Y**

```
UNTIL          X          OR          Y
```

Just like the Boolean data type in programming, Boolean variables are either **True** or **False**. X and Y will be either True or False. We equate True with 1 and False with 0 to represent electronic circuits being open or closed, just like with binary.

Circuit closed = 1 = True   Circuit open = 0 = False

Logic diagrams

Computers are based on electrical circuits where we can detect whether current is flowing or not. Binary uses base 2, so we have just two possible values 1 or 0. Representing data as binary values means we have to detect just two values in electrical circuits.

Binary logic is about these most basic circuits. Circuits in computers are made up of many logic gates but at this level we are looking at just three of them: **AND**, **OR** and **NOT**. A given input will generate an output based on the logic gate in use.

We use specific symbols to represent the different logic gates; these are standard symbols. They can be used to represent expressions such as Q = NOT A AND (B OR C).

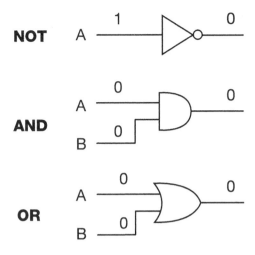

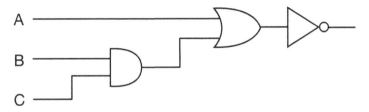

The logic gates can be joined up to make a circuit. For example NOT (A OR (B AND C))

Logic gates and truth tables

Each of the AND, OR and NOT gates can be represented by a truth table showing the output given each possible input or combination of inputs. Inputs are usually given algebraic letters such as A, B and C and output is usually represented by P or Q.

4

NOT gate

The NOT gate is represented by the symbol below and inverts the input. The small circle denotes an inverted input. If A is 1 (True), then NOT A is 0 (False).

Using 1s and 0s as inputs to a gate, its operation can summarised in the form of a **truth table**.

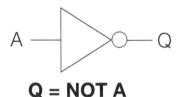

Q = NOT A

Input A	Output Q
0	1
1	0

The Boolean algebraic expression is written: $Q = \overline{A}$ where the overbar represents NOT.

AND gate

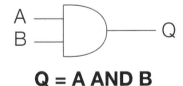

Q = A AND B

Input A	Input B	Output Q
0	0	0
0	1	0
1	0	0
1	1	1

The Boolean expression for AND is written: $Q = A \bullet B$ where $\bullet$ represents AND.

The truth table reflects the fundamental property of the AND gate: the output of A AND B is 1 (True) only if input A and input B are both 1 (True).

OR gate

Q = A or B

Input A	Input B	Output Q
0	0	0
0	1	1
1	0	1
1	1	1

The Boolean expression for OR is written: Q = A + B where + represents OR.

If A = 0 (False) and B = 0 (False) then A OR B = 0 (False), otherwise A OR B = 1 (True).

Combining logic gates into logic circuits

These logic gates can be combined to form more complex logic circuits which can carry out a number of functions. They are the basic building blocks of many electronic circuits found in computer memories, household devices, computer management systems in cars, and so on. Two examples are shown below. You should look at each logic circuit and follow the accompanying truth table which represents the logic circuit.

Example 1

The logic circuit below represents the Boolean condition (NOT A AND B) OR (A AND C). The outputs at D and E have been labelled so that they can be referred to in the truth table below the logic diagram.

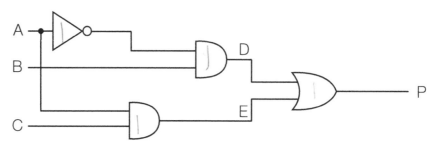

The truth table representing the above logic circuit:

A	B	C	NOT A	D = NOT A AND B	E = A AND C	P = D OR E
0	0	0	1	0	0	0
0	0	1	1	0	0	0
0	1	0	1	1	0	1
0	1	1	1	1	0	1
1	0	0	0	0	0	0
1	0	1	0	0	1	1
1	1	0	0	0	0	0
1	1	1	0	0	1	1

Interpreting the results of a truth table

Looking at the results of the truth table above, we can find out what the output will be for any combination of inputs.

For example, if A = 1, what other input must be 1 for the output to be 1?

If A = 0 and B = 1, what will be the output? Does it make a difference what the input C is? From the table, you can see that the output will be 1 whatever the value of C.

Q1 Complete the truth table for the following logic diagram:

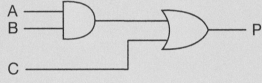

A	B	C	D = A AND B	P = D OR C
0	0	0		
0	0	1		
0	1	0		
0	1	1		
1	0	0		
1	0	1		
1	1	0		
1	1	1		

4

Q2 Figure 1 is a circuit diagram.

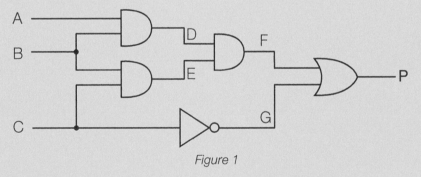

Figure 1

Complete the truth table for Figure 1.

A	B	C	D = A AND B	E = B AND C	F = D AND E	G = NOT C	P = F OR G
0	0	0					
0	0	1					
0	1						
0	1						
1							
1							
1							
1							

Example 2

A fish farm monitors the quality and level of the water. An alarm signal P (P = 1) is sent to the monitoring centre when certain conditions are detected. The inputs are:

Input	Binary value	Condition
N	1	Nutrient level < 10
	0	Nutrient level ≥ 10
T	1	Temperature ≥ 15
	0	Temperature < 15
L	1	Water level ≥ 4
	0	Water level < 4

The alarm signal is sent if **either** nutrient level < 10 AND temperature < 15

or temperature ≥ 15 AND water level < 4

Complete the truth table for this alarm system.

Solution:

The first condition is N = 1 AND T = 0. Write this as N AND NOT T

The second condition is T = 1 AND L = 0. Write this as T AND NOT L

The circuit diagram is then as shown below:

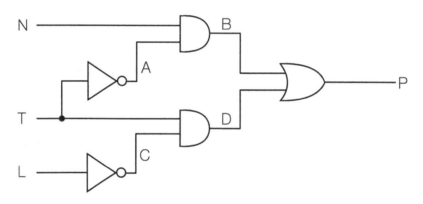

The partially completed truth table is:

N	T	L	A = NOT T	B = N AND A	C = NOT L	D = T AND C	P = B OR D
0	0	0	1	0	1	0	0
0	0	1	1				
0	1						
0	1						
1							
1							
1							
1							

Q3 Complete the truth table above.

4.2 Application and system software

Hardware and software

A computer system is made up of **hardware** and **software**. Hardware is any physical component that makes up the computer. Software is any program that runs on the computer.

Computer systems are all around us. They are not just the PCs on the desk but include mobile phones, cash machines, supermarket tills and the engine management systems in a modern-day car.

Software

Software is any program that runs on a computer. It can be grouped into two main categories:

- **System software**
  Programs that are needed to enable the computer to function, including the operating system, utilities, library routines and programming language translators.

- **Application software**
  Programs that enable a user to perform a task: that is, something that the user needs to do such as write an essay, keep a set of class marks, record pupil attendance or process orders.

Examples of application software include word processing software, spreadsheets, databases, games, mobile phone 'apps' and thousands of programs written for specific applications such as school registration, payroll, accounts, air traffic control and so on.

Operating system software

The operating system is a group of programs that manages the computer's resources. It manages all applications running on the computer. These include the management of:

- processor(s)
- memory
- input/output devices
- applications
- security

Processor management

The operating system manages the use of the processor resources. In a multi-tasking system such as Windows, several tasks may be running simultaneously. You can access the Task Manager by pressing **Ctrl-Alt-Del** to see what tasks are currently running on your PC.

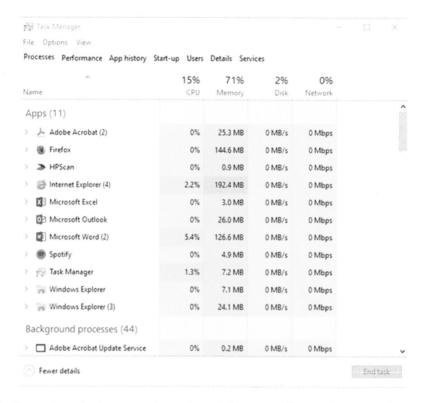

In actual fact, the various tasks are not running at the same time – the operating system allocates each one a tiny slice of processor time in turn. If, for example, the user is typing a document and pauses to think what to write next, the operating system will allocate the next task to the processor. If a long program is executing, it will only be allowed a few microseconds at a time (a time slice) before the processor moves to the next job.

Some computers have more than one processor core (see Section 4.4), and in that case, the operating system has to allocate tasks to each of them whenever possible. For example, different processor cores may be used to browse different websites that are currently loaded into memory.

Memory management

When a program is running it must be in the computer's main memory, and the operating system must manage where in memory each program and the data it needs will go. Most computers are capable of holding several programs in memory at the same time, so that a user can switch from one application to another.

When you start up a program (say, a Python program or any application software such as Word or Excel), the memory manager allocates it adequate blocks of free space in main memory.

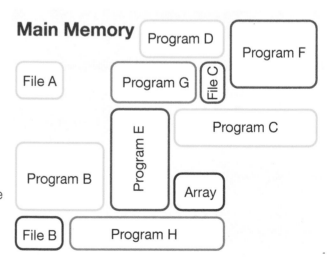

It also allocates memory for any data file that you open such as the essay you are working on in Word. When the program finishes or no longer needs the data in previously allocated memory blocks, the memory management system frees up that space for reuse.

Management of input/output devices

Input devices take real world data and convert it into a form that can be stored on the computer. The input from these devices is processed and the computer system will generate outputs. The **input device** could be, for example, a mouse, keyboard, microphone or sensor. The **output device** could be a conventional computer screen, an actuator that opens or closes a greenhouse window, or the speaker that produces sound on a phone.

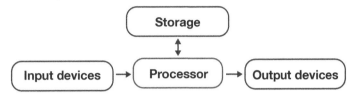

A function of the operating system is to manage these devices. When a user gives an instruction to print, the I/O management function takes over and controls the sending of the data to be printed from memory to the device driver. (Each input or output device has its own **device driver** – a small program that acts as an interface between the computer and the device. An HP printer, for example, will have different device drivers for a PC and a Mac, and the correct driver has to be installed so that the computer can communicate with the printer.) Meanwhile, the user can carry on editing their document in Word or whatever they were doing.

Application management

Application programs need an operating system to function. When you install a new application on your computer, the operating system will run a program to install it.

Installing an application

The user can, for example, choose to install the software in the default destination or change the folder, and the OS will respond accordingly.

The OS will interact with applications through an **Applications Program Interface (API)**, which allows the application to communicate with the operating system. Once an application is installed, it will need to communicate with the operating system to execute modules, save, update or delete data, and so on. The OS will maintain a directory of where each application and each data file is stored on disk.

When an application is run, the OS will allocate space in memory for it to be loaded and the job will enter the queue of jobs being allocated processor time.

4

Security management

Operating system security includes many methods to ensure safety from threats and attacks. Functions include:

- Controlling access to a computer by setting up passwords for different users. Without the password someone else will not be able to access the software applications and files on your computer

- Setting different access rights and privileges for different users

- Automatically downloading updates for the OS to ensure security loopholes are patched

- Encrypting files that are stored on the hard disk.

On a network, the operating system security software can also identify all the active users currently on the network, manually log out users and monitor when and for how long each user is logged in over a period of time.

> **Q4** Why might a network manager want to know when and for how long each user is logged in over a period of time?

Embedded systems

Many devices in the home use microprocessors/CPUs to control their functions. These are referred to as **embedded systems**. The control devices are usually on a single microprocessor stored within the device. They very often don't need an operating system since the tasks are usually simple and repeated and the input is usually done by pressing a button or setting a control. Examples of items that use this technology include: vehicles, cameras, medical equipment, aircraft, vending machines, microwave ovens, fridges, televisions, lifts/elevators and traffic lights.

Unlike the software in a PC or other type of non-embedded system:

- The system is held in non-volatile memory such as ROM or EPROM (Erasable Programmable Read-Only Memory) and is rarely if ever changed during the lifetime of the device

- Some firmware devices are permanently installed and cannot be changed after manufacture

- It is not usually possible to upgrade the hardware or attach peripherals.

The advantages of such technology are that it makes devices easier to use whilst also increasing reliability and offering features which enhance their usability.

Many embedded systems can connect to the Internet (usually using a **Wi-Fi** link) and can exchange data with the manufacturer's website or with the user. These so-called intelligent devices also allow users to set up a satellite box to start remotely recording a television programme or control their central heating system using an app on their smart phone.

Smart meters currently being installed in 26 million homes across Britain measure the gas and electricity you are using and display this on the screen of a handheld device. The smart meters also send automatic meter readings to the energy supplier using wireless technology, so that everyone will get accurate rather than estimated bills every month without any need to read the meter.

Q5 Describe in detail **four** of the functions of a typical operating system. Explain why certain household devices may not need to have an operating system.

Utility software

Strictly speaking the operating system is the software that controls and manages the computer system but most operating systems also include programs called **utilities**. Utilities are not essential for the computer to work but either make it easier for the user to use in some way, or provide housekeeping functionality. These utilities include:

- Security utilities that keep your data safe e.g. encryption software
- Disk organisation utilities that organise your files into folders and tidy up the disk
- Data compression utilities
- File backup utilities

Encryption software

Encryption tools can help to keep sensitive data safe from cyber-criminals or unauthorised access. They also protect backup copies of data kept on offline storage. Copies of sensitive information stored on flash memory sticks or laptops and removed from the office could be vulnerable to carelessness or theft. Encrypting the data will make sure it does not fall into the wrong hands.

The encryption process uses an algorithm and a key to transform **plaintext** into **ciphertext**. To decode the original information (the plaintext), it would be necessary to know both the algorithm and the key.

Maintenance utilities

Disk defragmentation

The file management utility above makes the secondary storage look like a nicely organised filing cabinet but it doesn't really look like this. Files are stored on the hard disk in blocks wherever there is space. If you have a big file it might get split up into segments so it can be stored in the available gaps. This isn't very efficient because the operating system then has to keep track of where all the segments are. After a while, thousands of files are stored in segments all over the disk. Files have become 'fragmented'.

The disk defragmenter moves the separate parts of the files around so that they can be stored together, which makes them quicker to access. The defragmenter also groups all the free disk space together so that new files can be stored in one place. This optimises disk performance.

Before disk is defragmented, the disk contains lots of files, stored all over the disk.

New file has to be saved in three different parts of the disk. Makes reading the file slower.

After defragmenting, the disk looks like this:

New file can be saved in one place so speeds up read access

Automatic updating

The automatic update utility makes sure that any software installed on the computer is up-to-date. For any software already installed on the computer, the automatic update utility will regularly check the Internet for updates. These will be downloaded and installed if they are newer than the version already on the computer.

Firewalls and antivirus software must be updated regularly as new viruses and threats are constantly being devised and discovered.

Application software should also be updated as there will be bug fixes and improvements that become available to people with a licence for that package.

Compression software

Compression software such as WinZip will reduce the size of a file. There are two types of compression known as lossy and lossless; lossy compression can be used on photos where some detail is lost but this will be undetectable when viewed. Lossless compression is used on text files, where it has to be possible to restore the file exactly (see Section 3.6).

Zipped or compressed files can be transmitted much more quickly over the Internet. Sometimes there is a limit to the size of a file which can be transmitted – if you have a 15Mb photograph, you will not be able to email it to a friend if there is a 10Mb limit on the attachments they can receive. Even if they can receive the file, it may take several minutes to download if they do not have a fast broadband connection.

4.3 Systems architecture

Von Neumann architecture

With the very first computers, it was not possible to store programs, and programs were generally input by setting switches. John Von Neumann developed the concept of the stored program computer in the 1940s. In the **Von Neumann** architecture:

- the program is stored in main memory and instructions are fetched and executed sequentially
- there is a single memory (and bus system) for accessing both data and programs.

Components of the processor

The processor responds to and processes the instructions that drive the computer. It contains the **Arithmetic Logic Unit (ALU), Control Unit (CU)**, **clock** and **bus**.

Arithmetic and Logic Unit (ALU)

The ALU carries out the following functions:

- **Logical operations:** These include AND, OR and NOT
- **Shift operations:** The bits in a computer word can be shifted left or right by a certain number of places
- **Arithmetic operations:** These include addition, subtraction, multiplication and division.

Control Unit

The Control Unit coordinates all the activities taking place inside the CPU. Its functions may be summarised as follows:

- It controls the execution of instructions in the correct sequence
- It decodes instructions
- It regulates and controls processor timing using regular pulses from the system **clock**
- It sends and receives control signals to and from other devices within the computer.

Clock

The system clock controls processor timing, switching between zero and one at rates exceeding several million times per second. It synchronises all CPU operations.

The clock frequency is the number of clock cycles which occur each second.

Bus

The CPU has internal connections or buses which pass data between the components of the CPU. As well as the ALU, Control Unit and clock, there are several fast memory locations called special-purpose registers which are involved in the Fetch-Execute cycle. Data and instructions are passed between registers and other components along these buses (which are referred to collectively as the bus.)

The system bus

The program instructions and data move between the main memory and the processor using internal connections called **buses**. The collection of wires or buses connecting the system components is known collectively as the **system bus**.

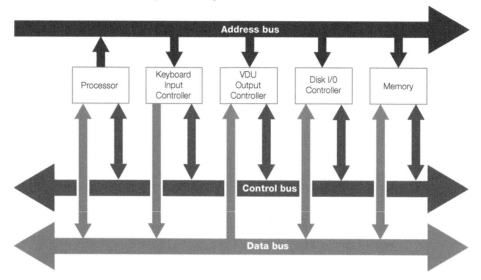

4.4 The CPU and Fetch-Execute cycle

Fetch-Execute cycle

When a program is to be run (executed) on a computer it first has to be loaded into main memory. From here it can be accessed by the processor, which runs each instruction in turn. When the program is loaded, the processor is given the start address of where it is held in main memory. To run the program the processor fetches an instruction, decodes it and then executes it. The processor executes one instruction at a time. This is called the **fetch-execute cycle**.

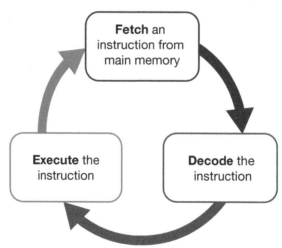

In the **fetch** part of the cycle:

- The address A of the next instruction to be executed is fetched from the register (a special fast memory location in the processor) where it is held

- This register is incremented so it points to the next instruction to be fetched

- The instruction at address A is fetched from memory and put into a special register ready to be decoded

In the **decode** part of the cycle:

- The Control Unit decodes the instruction to see what has to be done next

In the **execute** part of the cycle:

- The instruction is executed. Depending on what the instruction is, this could, for example, involve fetching data from memory and loading or adding it into the register, or jumping to another instruction in the program.

Factors affecting CPU performance

Clock speed

All processor activities begin on a clock pulse, although some activities may take more than one clock cycle to complete. One clock cycle per second = 1 Hertz (Hz), and clock speed is measured in Gigahertz (GHz), one billion cycles per second. Typical speeds for a PC are between 2 and 4 GHz. The greater the clock speed, the faster instructions will be executed.

Type and size of cache memory

One bottleneck that can occur is the access speed of main memory. Reading from and writing to main memory is much slower than the speed at which the processor can work. The logical answer is to use faster memory technologies but this increases the price of the computer. Modern computers need to run many programs at the same time so they need lots of memory. There needs to be a compromise between speed and cost.

One way of improving speed at minimal cost is to use a small amount of much faster memory called cache (pronounced "cash") where frequently used instructions or data can be stored temporarily.

Cache memory is an intermediary between the main physical RAM and the CPU. The **cache** makes any data frequently used by the CPU available much more quickly. Because the processor has to access main memory less often, it can work faster, so the CPU performance increases. If the required information is not located in the cache, it has to be fetched from main memory.

A typical PC (in January 2016) might have 4GB of RAM (main memory) but only 2MB of the faster more expensive cache memory. Notice the different units here and remember that there are 1000 Megabytes in a Gigabyte. This computer therefore has 2000 times more RAM than cache memory.

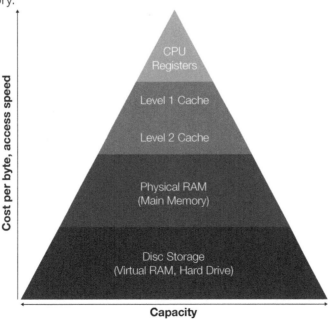

Cache can be used to either store instructions, data or both. The more cache memory a computer has, the more data and instructions can be held in cache and made available very quickly. This improves processor performance.

There are different 'levels' of cache:

- Level 1 cache is extremely fast but small (between 2-64KB)

- Level 2 cache is fairly fast and medium-sized (256KB-2MB)

- Some CPUs also have Level 3 data cache

Sometimes data and instructions are separated into different caches.

> Q6   Explain how clock speed and cache memory size can affect the performance of a computer.

> Q7   Which type of memory is the most expensive?

Processor cores

When we looked at the basic fetch-execute cycle we assumed that there was a single processor and a single main memory. You have probably heard the terms **dual-core** and **quad-core** so where do these fit in?

Today's more complex CPUs can include more than one core. A dual-core processor has two processing components within the CPU and a quad-core has four. In theory having two cores means that the computer can operate twice as fast but this isn't always the case.

A program is a series of instructions that need to be done in order. Multiple cores could work on different programs that operate in parallel but unless the program is designed to use multiple cores it isn't necessarily four times faster. On the whole though, a PC with a multi-core processor, executing many tasks at the same time, will operate faster than a single-core processor.

4.5 Memory

Memory and storage devices can be split up into two distinct groups:

- Main memory

- Secondary storage

Main memory can be accessed directly by the CPU, whereas secondary storage cannot. Data and instructions first have to be read from storage into memory.

Random Access Memory (RAM)

RAM is used to hold programs currently being executed, and the data the programs are using. When a program is to be executed, it has to be loaded from the hard disk into main memory so that the processor can access the instructions. Any data needed for that program to run is also loaded into main memory. The processor cannot access secondary storage directly. The main purpose of RAM is to act as temporary storage for programs and data while the program is being executed.

Volatility

When you are in the middle of a piece of work and there is a power failure or the computer is accidentally unplugged, you will notice that you lose the work you did since you last saved. This is because the saved version was copied onto the hard disk or solid state device, but the most recent version was only in RAM when the power went off. RAM is described as **volatile**; it loses its contents if there is no power. Hard disks and solid state devices are designed for long term storage of files and are **non-volatile** memory.

Read Only Memory (ROM)

RAM is volatile so when you turn off your computer it loses its contents. When you turn the computer back on it needs to get the basic startup routine from somewhere that is not volatile. The operating system and all your programs will be stored on the HDD/SSD but these need to be loaded into RAM to run.

The computer has a piece of software called the **bootstrap loader**. This is a small program that loads the operating system. Once the operating system is loaded it takes care of the rest. The term comes from the idea that when you're not doing very well in life you can "pull yourself up by your bootstraps". Bootstrapping became abbreviated to booting, a term you have probably heard before. To "boot" a computer is to start it up from scratch.

ROM is **Read Only Memory**; you cannot write over the contents once it has been created. It is also non-volatile; you can leave the computer switched off for months and it will still start up as soon as it has power again. RAM on the other hand is only used for temporary storage of programs when they are running.

RAM	ROM
Volatile – data is lost when the power is turned off (temporary memory)	Non-volatile – data is NOT lost when power is turned off (permanent memory)
Stores user data/programs/part of operating system which is currently in use	Used to store the BIOS/bootstrap loader which is required at start-up of the computer
Memory can be written to or read from	Memory can only be read from but NOT written to

4.6 Secondary storage

We all want to store files for a long period of time. We keep photographs, projects, music, films, letters and spreadsheets on our computers. We also expect our programs to be there when we switch the computer on. This long term storage is usually called secondary storage (primary storage is the main memory). **Secondary storage** refers to hard disk drives (HDDs), optical disks and more recently, Solid State Drives (SSDs).

Secondary storage devices

Secondary storage is **non-volatile**, generally holds much more data than main memory and is relatively inexpensive per MB. However, secondary storage technologies tend to have slower access speeds than main memory.

Secondary storage needs to be robust and reliable. Has your memory stick been through the washing machine yet?

Choosing a storage device

Choosing the right type of storage medium for a particular use is important. You need to consider the following features:

- **Capacity:** How much space is there to store files? A memory stick holding 8GB costs under £10 – how many high-resolution photos each of 10MB can you store on it?

- **Speed:** How quickly can the computer read data from a storage device or write data to it?

- **Portability:** Can you easily unplug it and carry it away? Does it fit in a pencil case or do you need a large bag? (When you write to an external hard disk or memory stick, you should use the little utility program that tells you whether or not the device can be safely removed from the computer before you remove it, or you may lose some data.)

> ℹ Safe To Remove Hardware ⚒ ✕
> The 'USB Mass Storage Device' device can now be safely removed from the computer.

- **Durability:** How easily is it damaged? Will it survive dropping or having coffee tipped on it?

- **Reliability:** How long will it last? Anything with moving parts is likely to be less reliable.

Magnetic disks

Magnetic disks are read with a moving head inside the disk drive. Moving parts make these media quite slow to read from or write to and also make the disk more susceptible to damage. This is in contrast to solid state media (SSD) which have no moving parts. Magnetic media are also vulnerable to magnetic fields. Just as a credit card with a magnetic strip left on a stereo speaker can be damaged by the magnets, so too a magnetic disk can be wiped by the magnetic fields in speakers.

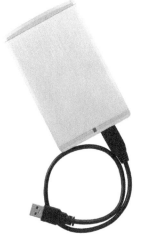

A hard disk uses rigid rotating platters coated with magnetic material. Ferrous (iron) particles on the disk are polarised to become either a north or south state. This represents 0 and 1. The disk is divided into tracks in concentric circles, and each track is subdivided into sectors. The disk spins very quickly at speeds of up to 10,000 RPM. Like an old record player, a drive head (like the needle on a record player) moves across the disk to access different tracks and sectors. Data is read or written to the disk as it passes under the drive head. When the drive head is not in use, it is parked to one side of the disk in order to prevent damage from movement. A hard disk may consist of several platters, each with its own drive head.

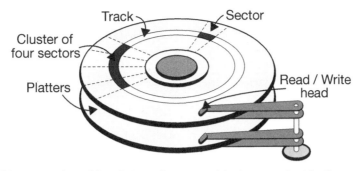

Magnetic disk drives can be either internal or portable (connected to the computer using a USB port).

Although hard disks are less portable than optical or solid state media, their huge capacity makes them very suitable for desktop purposes. Smaller, denser surface areas spinning under the read-write heads mean that newer disks have capacities of several terabytes.

The following table compares the two types of hard disk:

	Internal Hard Disk	Portable Hard Disk
Physical size of disk	3.5 inches	2.5 inches
Cost	3TB for £85	
Capacity	Up to 6TB	Up to 1.2TB
Access Speed	3Gb/s	640MB/s (5Gb/s) *(Speed of USB3 interface)*
Portability	Not portable, built into PC	Can fit in a large pocket
Durability	Good durability when disk not in use but vulnerable to movement when spinning. Can write to the disk an infinite number of times. Affected by heat and magnetic fields	
Reliability	Extremely reliable	
Typical use	Inside a PC as secondary storage	Supplementary storage for a PC or portable storage where high capacity is required

Solid state devices

Solid State Drives (SSD) have no moving parts and don't rely on magnetic properties, so are unaffected by magnetic fields. They are often referred to as **flash memory/storage**, but their access speeds are not as fast as RAM.

Solid state technology is also used in memory sticks (pen drives) and memory cards (e.g. SD and XD as used in cameras). Solid state technology is now also employed in many laptops and tablets as well as in mobile phones and other portable devices. Small size, non-volatile memory and reliability are key features in such devices which need to be portable and also have minimum drain on their internal batteries.

Inside a solid state drive

FLASH STORAGE DEVICES		
	Internal Solid State/ Flash Storage	USB Memory Stick	Memory Card
Cost	128GB for £40 960GB for £200	32GB for £15 128GB for £35	128GB SD card £25
Capacity	128GB to 2TB	16MB to 256GB	2GB to 128GB
Access Speed	6Gb/s *(faster than magnetic disk because no moving parts)*	640Mb/s *(speed of USB3 interface)*	*Dependent on type of card and device interface*
Portability	Not portable, built into PC	Very small, can put in any pocket or on a key-ring	Very small, designed for portable devices
Durability	More robust than hard disks with moving parts. Said to be 5-10 times more durable than a hard disk drive	Very durable. Some can be snapped quite easily	Very durable - not sensitive to temperature or knocks
Typical use	Notebooks, tablets, slim laptops	Personal use, moving files between computers	In phones and cameras

How solid state drives work

Solid state devices such as SSDs, memory sticks and memory cards all use **flash memory**. They are built from special types of transistors that do not lose their state when the power is switched off. There are two types of flash memory, **NOR** and **NAND**, which are wired in parallel and series respectively.

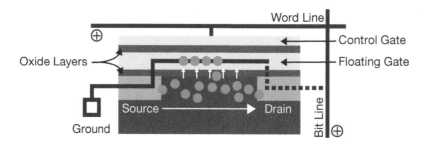

Both types of SSD use electrical circuits to persistently store data.

Q8 Which are cheaper, HDDs or SSDs? Is there a big difference in price? Which has the larger capacity?

Optical devices

Optical media includes CD, DVD and Blu-Ray disks.

	OPTICAL STORAGE DEVICES		
	CD	**DVD**	**Blu-Ray**
Cost	50 x 700MB CD-R for £14 (7p each)	50 x 4.7GB DVD-R for £12 (24p each)	50 x 25GB Blu-Ray for £22 (44p each)
Capacity	650MB	4.7GB (single layer) 8.5GB (dual layer) Double these capacities are possible for double-sided DVDs	25GB (single layer) 50GB (dual layer) Double these capacities are possible for double-sided disks
Access Speed	Up to 7.6 MB/s (52x)	16 MB/s (12x)	50 MB/s (12x)
Portability	Easy to carry in a large pocket or bag	Easy to carry in a large pocket or bag	Easy to carry in a large pocket or bag
Durability	Manufacturer's life expectancy is 10 to 25 years – but more realistically, 2-5 years		Manufacturer's life expectancy is 20 to 100 years – but the format may be outdated in 10-15 years
Reliability	Can be corrupted or damaged easily by excessive sunlight or scratches		
Typical use	CD-ROM for software distribution CD-R or CD-RW for backup/archive	DVD is used as a back-up device but also for distribution of software, games and the storage of movies	Blu-Ray used for storing of movies and games but also as a back-up device; very large storage capacity means it is replacing dvds

CDs come in three different formats: read-only (CD-ROM), recordable (CD-R) and rewriteable (CD-RW). CD-ROM, DVD and BluRay disks are 'pressed' with the pits and lands representing the data at the time of manufacture.

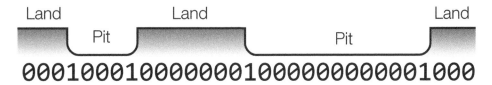

An optical disk works by using a low-powered laser to read the disk by bouncing light onto its surface, which is covered in pits and lands. At the point where a pit starts or ends, light is scattered and therefore not reflected so well. A land, and the bottom of a pit reflects the light well. Non-reflective and reflective areas are read as 1s and 0s. There is only one single track on

4

an optical disk, arranged as a tight spiral. A recordable disk uses a higher powered laser to change the reflecting properties of a disk and thus make lands and pits.

A CD ROM holds about 650MB of data, whereas a Blu-Ray disk can hold 50GB. Although these disks do not vary in size, their added capacity is owing to the shorter wavelength in the laser they use. This creates much smaller pits, enabling a greater number to fit in the same space along the track and also means that the track can be more tightly wound, and therefore much longer.

Pits and Lands

Spiral track

Summary of advantages and disadvantages of solid state, optical and magnetic storage

	Solid state	Optical	Magnetic
Advantages	Reliable, less susceptible to shock and damage than HDDs as they have no moving parts Considerably lighter than HDDs (which makes them suitable for laptops, tablets and other modern devices) Faster access times than HDDs because they don't spin and data can be accessed instantaneously Lower power consumption, meaning that in a laptop, for example, battery life is extended Run much cooler than HDDs (these points also make them very suitable for laptop computers)	Cheap to produce Easy to send through the post for distribution purposes	Inexpensive, very high capacity, internal drives very reliable
Disadvantages	Currently more costly per GB than HDDs May deteriorate over time and not last as long as HDDs	Can be corrupted or damaged easily by excessive sunlight or scratches	Not very portable owing to moving parts, so can be damaged when carried or dropped and corrupted by magnetic fields

Cloud storage

Increasingly, users are choosing to store their data and software "in the cloud". **Cloud storage** refers to saving data in an off-site storage system maintained by a third party, for example Dropbox, Google or Microsoft. Instead of saving data on your computer's hard drive or other local storage device, you save it in a remote storage facility, and access it via the Internet.

There are several advantages to this form of storage:

- You can access the data from anywhere in the world

- You can share the data with other people in different locations

- Backup is no longer such an issue, as it is the responsibility of the provider to keep the data safe.

There are also some disadvantages:

- You are dependent on having an Internet connection in order to access your data

- Some users are concerned about security in the cloud, and whether their data could be attacked by a hacker.

The data is stored, usually on hard disks but increasingly on solid state drives, in remote locations in different countries.

One of Google's server rooms in Council Bluffs, Iowa, USA

Exercises

1. (a) State the output of each of the following logic gates for the inputs given. [3]

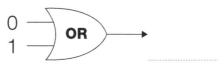

(b) Figure 1 is a circuit diagram.

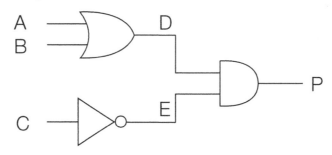

Figure 1

Complete the truth table for Figure 1. [3]

A	B	C	D = A OR B	E = NOT C	P = D AND E
0	0	0			
0	0	1			
0	1				
0	1				
1					
1					
1					
1					

2. Julian buys a new laptop with a **maintenance utility** and **security software** installed. Describe, using examples, the purpose of the maintenance utility and security software.

Maintenance utility: [1]

Purpose: [1]

Security software: [1]

Purpose: [1]

3. State which **four** of the tasks listed below are carried out by the operating system. [4]

   (a) Carrying out a spellcheck

   (b) Managing emails

   (c) Creating new folders on a storage device

   (d) Setting tab spaces

   (e) Multitasking

   (f) Organising hardware resources

   (g) Managing virtual storage

   (h) Sorting a database

4. Tick **one** box in each row to show whether each of the following statements is true or false. [5]

	True	**False**
All other things being equal, the higher the clock speed, the faster the speed of the processor		
The CPU fetches and decodes instructions		
Cache memory is slower than RAM		
If a CPU has many cores, this slows down the computer		
The speed of the CPU is usually measured in Gigahertz (GHz)		

4

5. (a) Describe **three** advantages of solid state drives compared with hard disk drives. [3]

   (b) Why might an organisation choose a hard disk drive rather than a solid state drive for their file server? [1]

   (c) Describe briefly the operation of a solid state drive. [3]

   (d) Describe briefly the operation of a hard disk drive. [3]

   (e) Explain what is meant by **cloud storage**. [2]

   (f) Give **three** advantages of cloud storage compared to local storage. [3]

6. A computer has 2,000 megabytes of RAM.

   (a) How many gigabytes of RAM does the computer have? [1]

   (b) State **two** items that will be stored in RAM. [2]

   (c) The computer also has 2MB of cache memory.

   Describe what is meant by cache memory and state why it is used. [3]

   (d) State **one** use of ROM in a computer. [1]

Section 5 – Fundamentals of computer networks

Objectives

- Define what a computer network is
- Discuss the benefits and risks of computer networks
- Describe the main types of computer network including PAN, LAN and WAN
- Understand that networks can be wired or wireless
- Discuss the benefits and risks of wireless networks as opposed to wired networks
- Explain star and bus network topologies
- Explain the term "network protocol"
- Describe the purpose and use of network protocols including Ethernet, Wi-Fi, TCP, UDP, IP, HTTP, HTTPS, FTP and email protocols SMTP, IMAP
- Understand the need for, and importance of, network security
- Explain the following methods of network security:
    - o authentication
    - o encryption
    - o firewall
    - o MAC address filtering
- Describe the 4 layer TCP/IP model:
    - o application layer
    - o transport layer
    - o network layer
    - o link layer
- Understand that the HTTP, HTTPS, SMTP, IMAP and FTP protocols operate at the application layer
- Understand that the TCP and UDP protocols operate at the transport layer
- Understand that the IP protocol operates at the network layer

5.1 Wired and wireless networks

A computer network is a collection of computers linked together to facilitate communication and the sharing of resources. They may be connected either wired or wirelessly.

The Internet

The largest and most famous wide area network in the world is the **Internet**, a collection of **inter-**connected **net**works. It is a worldwide collection of computers and networks, not owned or managed by any one group of people. Anyone can access the Internet.

The Internet is not the same thing as the World Wide Web. Websites are stored on web servers connected to the Internet, and each site has a unique web address so that it can be accessed. All information on the World Wide Web is stored in documents known as **web pages**. These pages are accessed using a program called a **web browser** such as Firefox, Mozilla or Google Chrome.

The Web is just one of the ways in which information is communicated over the Internet. The Internet, not the Web, is used for email and instant messaging.

Wide Area Networks

Wide area networks or **WANs** tend to be under collective or distributed ownership and are not necessarily owned by one organisation, owing to the extremely high cost of such a system. For example a group of government departments, NHS trusts or financial institutions might collectively own a wide area network.

Some large and medium-sized organisations have their own private wide area networks or WANs. A WAN is a collection of computers and networks connected together using resources supplied by a 'third party carrier' such as British Telecom. It uses cables, telephone lines, satellites and radio waves to connect the components, which are usually spread over a wide geographical area.

A business with offices in London, Leeds, Bristol and York may lease connections from a network service provider to connect the four office LANs together.

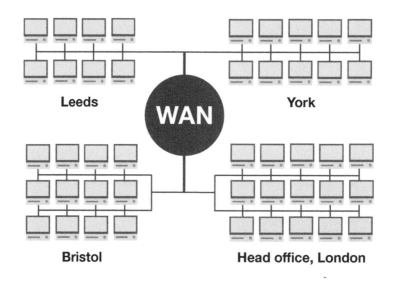

Data transmission

In order to communicate with other computing devices in a local or wide area network such as the Internet, various items of hardware are needed. First we'll look at how data is sent across the Internet.

Every device that can connect to the Internet has a separate, unique address known as its **IP (Internet Protocol) address**. A mobile device's IP address can change as it moves location, as its physical location needs to be known in order for it to receive communications.

Packet switching

Suppose you want to send a file of 3Mb across the Internet. The file is broken up into data **'packets'** of around 512 bytes. Each packet is given a header containing

- The IP (Internet Protocol) address it is going to
- The IP address it has come from
- The sequence number of the packet
- The number of packets in the whole communication
- Error checking data

Packets are then sent to their destination along different routes, and reassembled in the right order when they arrive.

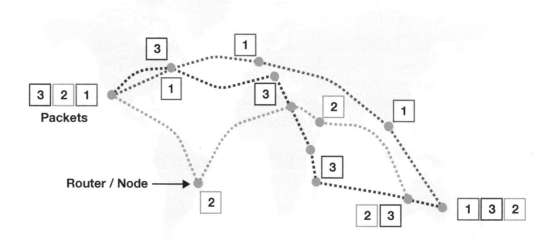

Network hardware

The hardware required to create a network of computers includes **routers**, **switches** and **Network Interface Cards (NICs)**.

Routers and switches

A **router** is designed to route data packets across a wide area network such as the Internet. Each router in a network acts as a node and packets are passed from router to router to their destination. If a packet is destined for a computer in a LAN, it will typically be routed to a **switch**.

A **switch** is a component of a LAN that knows the MAC addresses of each individual device connected to it locally. Its function is to send the packets only to the intended recipient, using its MAC address.

Network Interface Card (NIC)

A **Network Interface Card (NIC)** is required to connect any network-enabled device. This is a physical component which can either operate wirelessly or have a wired connection using a standard **Ethernet** cable. All devices that can connect to a network have an NIC including your home computer, a smartphone, an Internet-enabled light bulb or a network printer.

MAC addressing

Each NIC has a Media Access Control or **MAC address** assigned to it by the manufacturer. Your computer may have more than one MAC address – one for wired **Ethernet** and one for **wireless**. A mobile phone may have different MAC addresses for wireless and Bluetooth.

A MAC address is a 48-bit address that is written as twelve hex digits to make it easier for humans to work with. The first six digits (e.g. 00-1C-B3) are used to identify the manufacturer of the device – in this case, Apple Corporation. The second set of digits gives the serial number of the device. For example:

In hex: `00-1C-B3-F1-F7-85`

In binary: `0000 0000 0001 1100 1011 0011 1111 0001 1111 0111 1000 0101`

This is the MAC address of a device with serial number F1-F7-85 made by Apple.

Every networked device in the world has a unique, unchanging MAC address.

Wireless networking

Many networks use wireless fidelity (**Wi-Fi**) connections rather than physical wires. Wi-Fi is a family of **protocols** or rules that make wireless networking run smoothly.

Advantages of wireless networking

- Users can move around freely within the area of the network with their phones, laptops and handheld devices and get an Internet connection

- Users can share files and other resources connected to the network without having to be connected to a port

- It saves the expense, time and inconvenience of having to lay cables through walls, floors and ceilings

5

- It is easier to add new devices as no new cabling is required
- Instant transfer of data is much quicker – for example, you can take a photograph on a mobile device and upload it instantly to Facebook

Disadvantages of wireless networks

- File transfer speeds are generally slower with wireless connections
- Wireless connections can be obstructed by walls, ceilings and furniture
- Wireless networks are generally less secure and easier to hack into

Risks of wireless networks

Criminal activity – an unauthorised user can use the wireless connection to hack into the network and cause damage by planting viruses, or bring the network to a halt by flooding it with useless traffic (Denial of Service attack).

Bandwidth stealing – by using the Internet connection to download music, games and other software, outside intruders can slow the network down

Confidentiality – if any network information is not encrypted before transmission, an intruder can gain access to confidential information.

5.2 Network topologies and data transmission

Local Area Networks (LANs)

A **Local Area Network (LAN)** usually covers a relatively small geographical area. It consists of a collection of computers and peripheral devices (such as printers) connected together, often on a single site. At school you probably have many different buildings within a campus, with the school's LAN connecting the computers in all these buildings. A LAN is often owned and managed by a single person or organisation.

Benefits of Networking Computers

These are some of the benefits of networking computers belonging to a single organisation:

Sharing resources

- Folders and files can be stored on a file server so they can be accessed by authorised users from any computer on the network
- Peripheral devices such as printers and scanners can be shared
- Internet connection can be shared and any authorised user on the network can use email

Centralised management

- User profiles and security can all be managed centrally
- Software can be distributed across the network rather than having to install it on each individual computer
- All files can be backed up centrally

The disadvantages of networking computers include:

- If the file server goes down, no one can access their files or do any work
- Network faults could lead to loss of data
- As network traffic increases, performance degrades so accessing resources might be slow
- It is difficult to make the system secure from hackers
- Viruses may be able to infiltrate the network and infect every computer
- The larger the network becomes, the more difficult it is to manage

Network topologies

Computers can be connected together in different layouts, or **topologies**. Two common topologies are **star** and **bus**.

Star topology

All of the computers have their own cable connecting them to a **switch**, which routes messages to the correct computer. A powerful computer called the **server** controls the network.

Advantages:	Disadvantages:
If one cable fails the other workstations are not affected	Can be costly to install because there is a lot of cabling and extra hardware such as the switch
Consistent performance even when the network is heavily used	If the server or the central switch fails then the whole network goes down
Good security as data is received only by the node for which it is intended	

5

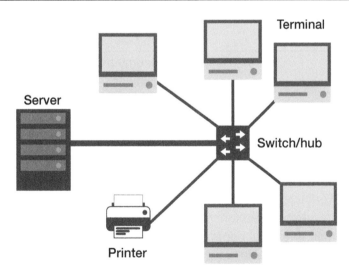

A star topology is often the layout of choice in a school or office because they are the most reliable of the topologies.

Bus topology

Historically, computers on a bus topology were connected to a single backbone cable. The computers all share this cable to transmit to each other, and each message is divided into **frames**. All the nodes (computing devices) receive all the data frames transmitted by any node. Each node then has to determine if the frame is to be accepted, using its unique identifier or MAC address (see earlier in this Section). Only one computer can successfully transmit at any one time, which is fine most of the time if the network is not too busy but if there is a lot of traffic then transmissions interfere with each other and computers have to retransmit. As the number of collisions increased, the network slows down.

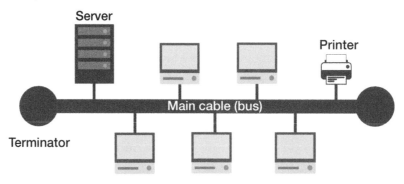

Advantages:	Disadvantages:
Easy and inexpensive to install – less cabling than in a star topology	If the main cable fails then the whole network goes down
No reliance on a central node	Cable failures are hard to isolate because all of the computers in the network are affected
	Performance slows down as the amount of traffic increases
	Low security as every node can see all the transmissions

A bus topology of this kind is a good choice for a temporary network in a single room, since it can be easily constructed with a minimum of cabling and extra hardware, and easily dismantled.

Personal Area Networks (PANs)

A **PAN** is a computer network used for data transmission among devices such as computers, cell phones and laptops. A PAN can be used for communication between the devices themselves or for connecting to the Internet. The most common kind of technology used in a wireless PAN is **Bluetooth**, which uses short-range radio waves over distances up to approximately 10 metres.

For example, Bluetooth devices such as keyboards and printers can connect wirelessly to a computer, mobile phone or tablet provided they are within a few metres of each other.

Ethernet

Ethernet refers to a family of networking rules or **protocols** widely used in Local Area Networks (LANs).

It describes how devices should format data ready for transmission between computers on the same network.

- Similar to polite human conversation, nodes will wait until the connection is quiet before attempting to 'speak' or transmit

- Two nodes attempting to transmit simultaneously will stop and each wait a random period before reattempting

All new computers have Ethernet built in, and old machines can be retro-fitted. Almost every reference to "network ready," "LAN" or "LAN connection" implies use of the Ethernet system.

Transmission media

The standard network cable is often referred to as an Ethernet cable. It uses twisted-pair copper cabling or fibre optics.

Which cable should be used?

Connecting computers with copper cable is cheaper, as most PCs come with built-in copper Network Interface Cards (NICs). Optical NICs cost around £100 each.

Copper cable offers advantages in rural areas where it may already be used in telephone networks. Using the existing cable will save the cost of running new cable throughout a site for a LAN. For most applications the speed of copper cable is adequate so the lower associated cost of NICs and routing equipment mean it is widely used, especially in LANs.

However, in many situations fibre optic is the cable of choice. It has much greater bandwidth, transmission is faster and the cables do not break as easily as copper cables. They are not affected by electromagnetic interference, unlike copper cables which can interfere with other wires and cause lost or distorted transmissions over a network. Over a distance of 100 metres, fibre optic cable loses only 3% of signal strength, whereas copper cable loses 94% over the same distance and will need repeaters or boosters over that distance.

Ethernet transmission

Ethernet systems divide data into **frames**, similar to Internet packets. Each frame contains source and destination MAC addresses and error checking data. In the older, traditional bus networks, frames are broadcast to all nodes, and only the intended recipient will open the frame. More modern bus networks operate with a switch which routes the frames directly to the correct device. Faulty frames containing transmission errors are dropped or resent.

5

5.3 Network security

Networks are more vulnerable to hackers than standalone devices since a hacker may access a network through one device in order to gain access to other devices on the same network. This could have serious implications for an organisation, resulting in data theft, corruption of data, denial of service, and other damage caused by malware being installed on network servers.

Security on a network is important to prevent unauthorised access to data, misuse or modification of data including installing viruses and other malware.

Methods of keeping a network secure

Network security has two basic goals:

- To keep unauthorised people from accessing resources
- To ensure that authorised people *can* access the resources they need

Methods used to maintain network security include:

- Authentication
- Encryption
- Firewall
- MAC address filtering

Authentication

There are a number of ways of identifying a genuine, authorised user.

Password Protection

In a networked environment such as a school or a company, many of the computers are used by more than one person. Even if employees have their own computer it may be in an open plan office. The easiest way to stop unauthorised access to your computer or your files is to use a combination of a username and password.

The password should never be shared with friends or stuck on a post-it note under the keyboard (yes, people really do!). Also, the password should be "strong". This means that it is not easy to guess, it probably contains letters, numbers and symbols and is at least six characters long. Some companies make employees change their password every month, but this is not always effective because people may, for example, just add the month number on the end because it is easy to remember.

For additional security against people trying lots of different passwords to get into someone else's account, the account can be locked after a certain number of failed attempts.

User access levels

User access levels should be set for disks, folders and files so users can only access what they need to. At school you can probably read files on a shared area but not edit them; this is Read-Only access. The teacher will have Read-Write access to these folders. Some folders you won't even be able to see.

In a work environment, the Accounts staff will have access to payroll details but other departments will not. The Data Protection Act says that employers must keep personal data secure so setting appropriate access rights is a legal responsibility as well as a good idea.

Encryption

Encryption is used primarily to protect data and prevent it being hacked or accessed illegally. Data that is being transmitted over the Internet is vulnerable to hackers. For example, someone who uses an online shopping site will have to type in their payment details, such as a credit or debit card number, and it is essential that this information is kept secure. If they are paying by PayPal, they will have to type in their email address and password, which needs to be kept safe from anyone intercepting the transmission. Someone accessing their bank details needs to know that a hacker cannot steal this data.

Whilst encryption won't prevent hacking, it makes the data unreadable unless the recipient has the necessary decryption tools.

Encryption terminology

- **Plaintext:** the original message to be encrypted
- **Ciphertext:** the encrypted message
- **Encryption:** the process of converting plaintext into ciphertext
- **Decryption:** the process of converting ciphertext into plaintext
- **Key:** a sequence of numbers used to encrypt or decrypt, often using a mathematical formula
- **Encryption algorithm:** the method for encrypting the plaintext

A very simple example of encryption is the Caesar shift cipher, in which each letter is replaced by a letter *n* number of positions further on in the alphabet. The key in this case is *n*.

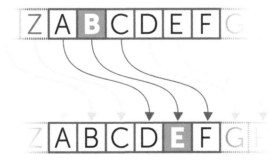

> **Q1** Given the key 5, decode the encrypted message KNWJHWFHPJW BNQQ QTXJ

5.3 **Network security** 119

Clearly this is not a very useful method of encryption in practice, since it is very easy to discover the key and decrypt the message. There are many methods of **strong encryption** which make the ciphertext virtually impossible to break.

Firewall

A **firewall** is primarily designed to prevent unwanted Internet traffic from gaining access to the LAN. Unauthorised users external to the network are blocked by the firewall, which can also block any attempts to gain access via certain ports used for restricted data transmission such

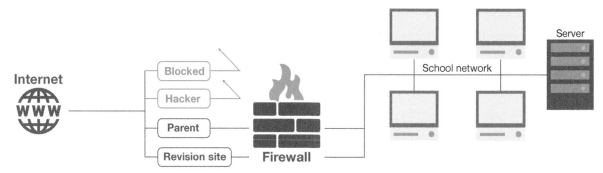

as FTP. Typical firewall mechanisms for doing this might include blocking data from certain IP addresses or on certain ports that indicated a type of traffic that was not wanted, such as an attempt to access FTP.

Operating systems like MS Windows have firewall utilities included but you can also buy firewall software separately. Free firewall software can also be downloaded from the Internet and many banks provide free firewall software to customers using their Internet banking services.

MAC address filtering

Every computing device has a unique MAC address, so it is possible to use MAC filtering on a wireless network to determine which devices are allowed access to the network. This has a weakness in that although it identifies the permitted devices, it does not identify which individual is using a device. That has to be done using a password or by using one of the other methods described above.

5.4 Protocols and layers

Protocols

If one computer transmits a stream of binary to another computer, the receiving end needs to know what the rules are. This is called a **protocol**. A protocol is the set of rules that define how devices communicate. A protocol will specify, for example:

* the format of data packets
* the addressing system
* the transmission speed
* error-checking procedures being used

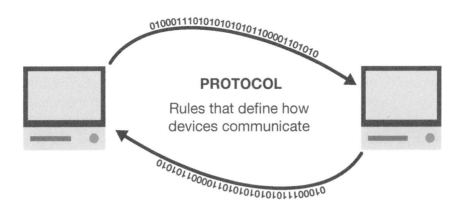

Ethernet protocol

The **Ethernet** protocol was described briefly in Section 5.1 as a family of related protocols. Ethernet stations communicate by sending each other data frames, individually sent and delivered. Each Ethernet station has a 48-bit MAC address and these addresses specify the source and destination of each frame.

Ethernet is now so universally used that most manufacturers build Ethernet interfaces directly onto PC motherboards, eliminating the need for a separate network card (NIC).

Wi-Fi

Wi-Fi is a trademark for the technology that allows electronic devices to connect to a wireless LAN (**WLAN**). Devices which can use Wi-Fi technology include personal computers, video-games consoles, smartphones, digital cameras and tablet computers. Wi-Fi compatible devices can connect to the Internet via a wireless LAN and a **Wireless Access Point (WAP).**

The WAP receives data from a network via its physical connection. The transmitter then converts this data into radio waves which are then transmitted. Any device on the network receives this radio signal via a Wi-Fi adaptor which allows it to communicate or download data from the data source. This also works in the reverse direction when a device wishes to send data over the network to another computer.

Laptop computer **Wireless access point** **Printer**

In 1999, the Wi-Fi Alliance was established to establish international standards for network connections.

Transmission Control Protocol/Internet Protocol (TCP/IP)

TCP/IP consists of two separate protocols. **TCP** is a standard that defines how messages are broken up into packets and reassembled at the destination. It also detects errors and resends lost packets. The **IP** protocol identifies the location of a device on the Internet and routes the individual packets from source to destination via **routers**.

User Datagram Protocol (UDP)

UDP uses a simple connectionless transmission model. With UDP, computer applications can send messages referred to as **datagrams** to other hosts on an IP network. It is an alternative to TCP but has no error checking or correction. UDP transmission also maintains an open connection between the sender and the recipient for the duration of the communication. For these reasons, two-way communication is often faster and consequently UDP is often used for online gaming sessions.

HyperText Transfer Protocol (HTTP) and HyperText Transfer Protocol Secure (HTTPS)

HTTP is used for accessing and receiving web pages in the form of HTML (Hypertext Markup Language) files on the Internet. The protocol requests the web server to transmit the requested web page to the user's browser for viewing.

HTTPS serves the same purpose as HTTP, but encrypts the information so that it cannot be understood if it is hacked. Banks always use the HTTPS protocol.

> **Q2** What other websites might require the use of https?

File Transfer Protocol (FTP)

This is a standard network protocol used when transferring computer files between a client and server on a computer network. FTP is based on a client-server model and uses separate control and data connections between the client and the server.

Email protocols

Mail servers pass on or store emails until they are collected. You must log on to a mail server to collect mail.

Internet Messaging Access Protocol (IMAP)

The Internet Message Access Protocol (IMAP) is an email protocol that stores email messages on a server but allows users to view and manipulate the messages as though they were stored locally on their own computers. Users can organise messages into folders, flag messages as urgent and save draft messages on the server.

Simple Mail Transfer Protocol (SMTP)

SMTP is a protocol for sending e-mail messages between servers. Most e-mail systems that send mail over the Internet use SMTP to send messages from one server to another; the messages can then be retrieved with an e-mail client using either POP or IMAP. Users typically use a program that uses SMTP for sending e-mail and either POP or IMAP for receiving e-mail. (POP is an alternative email protocol.)

SMTP's primary function is different from POP and IMAP. SMTP is used for sending out email from an email client. It is also used for relaying or forwarding mail messages from one mail server to another; this is necessary if the sender and recipient have different email service providers.

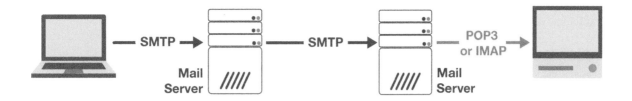

The concept of layers

The TCP/IP model consists of four **layers**, creating a modular design with each layer responsible for a small part of the communication process.

The advantage of this modular design is that it lets suppliers such as Microsoft easily adapt the protocol software to specific hardware and operating systems. For example, software for an Ethernet system can be adapted to an optical-fibre network by changing only the link layer – other layers are not affected.

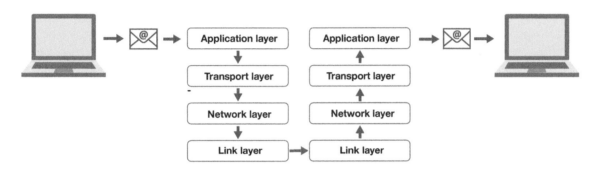

5

Packets of data are passed down through the layers which each perform their individual functions before it is transmitted across the network. At the receiving end, the packets are then passed back up through the layers to the application they are intended for.

- At the top there is the **Application layer** which is where the network applications, such as web browsers and email programs, operate. The data being sent is encoded so that it will be understandable by the recipient. This means formatting data and adding an appropriate header according to a protocol being used, such as **HTTP** (used by web browsers), **HTTPS**, **FTP**, **IMAP** and **SMTP**.

- Next there is the **Transport layer** which sets up the communication between the two hosts and establishes settings such as "language" and size of packets. It splits the data into packets and adds packet information such as the packet number specifying that packet's order and the total number of packets so they can be reassembled correctly. It hides different network technologies and architectures. **TCP** and **UDP** operate on this layer.

- The third layer is the **Network/Internet** Layer which addresses and packages data for transmission, and routes the packets across the network. It attaches the IP address of the sender so the recipient will know who sent it. It also attaches the destination IP address. **IP** operates on this layer.

- The fourth layer is the **Link layer** which is where network hardware such as the network interface card (NIC) is located. OS device drivers also sit here. It attaches the MAC addresses of the sender and the recipient, allowing the packet to be directed to a specific device on a local area network, for example.

Exercises

1. A small company with five employees has installed a Local Area Network (LAN).

    (a) Describe what is meant by a Local Area Network (LAN). [2]

    (b) The network has been connected using a star topology.

      Draw a diagram of the star topology. [2]

    (c) Give **two** advantages of a star topology in this scenario. [2]

    (d) A bus is another topology that can be used when creating a LAN.

      Draw a diagram of the bus topology. [2]

    (e) The company is organising a week-long exhibition at a large exhibition hall. They need to set up a temporary local area network (LAN). State, with reasons, what type of LAN you would recommend. [3]

2. (a) A wireless network can be set up using Wi-Fi connections. What is Wi-Fi? [1]

    (b) Give **two** advantages and **two** disadvantages of wireless networks compared with wired networks. [4]

3. (a) What is Bluetooth? [1]

    (b) Describe **one** difference between a PAN and a LAN. [1]

    (c) Give **three** advantages of using fibre optic cable over copper cable when connecting computers in a LAN. [3]

4. Several methods may be used to authenticate a user on a network.

    (a) Describe briefly **two** methods of authentication [4]

    (b) Describe briefly **two** other ways of keeping network data secure. [4]

5. (a) When two computers on a network communicate, they have to use the same **protocol**. What is a protocol? [1]

    (b) State which would be the most suitable protocol in each of the following situations. Select one in each case, from the following: TCP/IP   HTTP   HTTPS   FTP   IMAP   SMTP

      (i) Making a payment securely when purchasing something over the Internet [1]

      (ii) Transferring a file to another computer on a wide area network [1]

      (iii) Transferring an email from one server to another server [1]

    (c) Show on which layer each of these protocols operates:

      TCP, UDP, IP, HTTP, FTP, SMTP, IMAP

Layer	Protocol
Application	
Transport	
Network/Internet	
Link	

[7]

Section 6 – Fundamentals of cyber security

Objectives

- Define the term cyber security and be able to describe its main purposes
- Understand and be able to explain the following cyber security threats:
    - o malicious code
    - o weak and default passwords
    - o misconfigured access rights
    - o removable media
    - o unpatched and/or outdated software
- Explain what penetration testing is and what it is used for
- Define the term social engineering
- Describe what social engineering is and how it can be protected against
- Explain the following forms of social engineering:
    - o blagging
    - o phishing
    - o pharming
    - o shouldering (or shoulder surfing)
- Describe what malware is and how it can be protected against
- Describe the following forms of malware: computer virus, Trojan, spyware, adware
- Understand and explain the following security measures:
    - o biometric measures (particularly for mobile devices)
    - o password systems
    - o CAPTCHA (or similar)
    - o using email confirmation to confirm a user's identity
    - o automatic software updates

6

6.1 Cyber security threats

Cyber security consists of the processes, practices and technologies designed to protect networks, computers, programs and data from attack, damage or unauthorised access. It is defined as the protection of computer systems, networks and data from criminal activity. Cybercrime can take many forms, including planting viruses, acquiring and using personal or confidential data and disrupting a website or service.

Vulnerability of a computer network is often due to a flawed system which is open to attack. An attacker or hacker can then exploit this weakness.

Removable media

Removable media such as memory sticks and removable hard drives can pose two major threats to an organisation: **data theft** and **virus infection.**

Suppose you copy your latest school project on to a memory stick and take it home to use in your own computer. If your computer does not have adequate virus protection then the memory stick could become infected, and infect the whole school network when you insert it into a school computer.

Human error is one of the largest single factors in security breaches. For example, in 2010 GCHQ lost 35 laptops with all the security data stored on these devices; there are numerous similar cases reported on the Internet.

Many IT rules do not take into account the frailty of human nature. System users often don't believe that security rules refer to them in their everyday use of computer systems.

> **Q1** In one study carried out, researchers scattered several memory sticks in the car parks of a number of companies. Nearly 60% of workers who found these devices used them in their office computers without giving any consideration to potential security risks. The percentage of workers who used these devices actually rose to 90% when they saw an official logo printed on the device.
>
> What are the risks of using an unidentified memory stick in your computer?

Weak and default passwords

Even the use of passwords is no guarantee of security. On average, Internet users have about 25 applications or devices (e.g. phones and tablets) that they have to manage; research has shown that these users often only have five or six unique passwords covering all devices and applications.

When a device needs a username and password to log on, a **default password** is usually provided that allows the device to be accessed during setup. Some users are careless and do not change the default password that the designer of a system may have used for testing

How secure is my password?
Test the strength of your passwords

er87?HkFT+

Estimated Time To Crack: 19 Million Years
Recomendations: Good Job! All Character Types In Use
Strength Evaluation: Strong
Score: 80
Length of Password: 10
Attempts per second: 100,000

purposes, such as "password" or "admin". The default password is usually found in the instruction manual or on the device (e.g. a router) itself.

Leaving a default password is one of the major factors in compromising the security of a system.

A weak password is one that is easily guessed, such as a word from a dictionary or a piece of personal data that can easily be found out about the user. Lists of the most commonly used passwords are readily available on the Internet for any hacker trying to guess a password. They include: 12345, abc123, password, p@ssw0rd, admin, football, secret and monday.

Case study

In 2016 an heiress used the name of her dog as the password for her email account. She talked about the dog on several social media posts, and the account was hacked. When she went on holiday, they sent fake invoices to the family business for private jets, luxury villas and shopping sprees, which paid out around $900,000 before the crime was detected. It was only when her father got annoyed at how much money she was spending that it was discovered.

Misconfigured access rights

In an organisation such as a school or business, user names are used to identify the access rights for each user. Each user is assigned individual access rights, according to their role, and it is important that these should be set correctly. The starting position should be that for a new application, every option is turned off by default, and only features that are needed by a particular user or group of users should be turned on.

For example, most network users should not have access to setup and configuration pages, since a hacker who gains access to the user's computer could then cause damage.

As people change roles within an organisation or new roles are created, if these access rights are not carefully managed, they may create barriers to legitimate access or conversely, allow some people into areas which they should not have access to. This can create a security weakness.

Access rights can also be applied to individual files. This means that specific files, stored in an area to which full access is normally allowed, can still be given restrictions such as being made read-only.

Unpatched or outdated software

Software companies selling software such as operating systems, browsers, commercial applications packages and games are very alert to the possibility of their software being attacked by malware. In a 2015 review, it was found that 87% of vulnerabilities were 'patched' within 24 hours of being discovered. However, although users may be notified and offered a free software update, not every organisation or individual will automatically take up the offer.

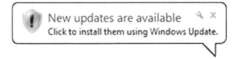

Of the known vulnerabilities in packages such as MS Office, Windows, Java and Adobe Reader, 44% were between two and four years old. The top ten vulnerabilities were all known and patched years ago.

Other cyber security threats including **social engineering** and **malicious code** are considered in the next two subsections.

6.2 Social engineering

People are often the weakest point in security systems and criminals have engineered methods to take advantage of human error and gullibility. It doesn't matter how many burglar alarms and double locks you have installed in your home, if you believe the robber who comes to the door and says he is there to check the electric meter.

Social engineering is the art of manipulating people so they divulge personal information such as passwords of bank account details. It is much easier to pretend to be trustworthy, and to fool an acquaintance or colleague into telling you personal information, than to try to secretly hack into their computer to find it out.

Social engineering includes the following techniques:

- blagging

- phishing

- pharming

- shouldering (shoulder surfing)

Blagging

Blagging is the act of "knowingly or recklessly obtaining or disclosing personal data or information without the consent of the controller" (owner of the data). For example, a dishonest employee may persuade a colleague to tell them private information such as their password, pretending that they need it in order to install some new software on their computer. This then gives them access to their computer files and could lead to a security breach or even identity theft.

To prevent blagging, the company should make sure that they provide **security training** to their employees so that they don't fall for these tricks.

This, of course, could also be used on social networking sites where people are tricked into giving out personal data which could lead to all kinds of problems.

Phishing

Phishing emails are designed to steal money, get login details, or steal an identity. You may receive an email inviting you to click on a link to download a free game or verify your bank account details. The criminal will then ask you to enter data such as a bank account number or password as well as personal details such as name, address, birth date and so on.

> **Halifax Bank Plc** (no-reply@home.ne.jp)
> To: recipients
>
> Hi,
>
> We're just checking this is the right email address for you.
>
> Soon your email address will become your username to access Halifax Account - that makes it easier than remembering yet another username.
>
> If this is the email address you want to use, all you have to do is click the link below
>
> https://my.halifax.co.uk/your-account/verify-email-details?verificationCode=eee96442-51d6-4868-b0f3-a5484447eae8

Once a hacker has your email address, they may be able to gain access to your contact list and if so, they can email your friends pretending to be you. The email may be an urgent request for help:

CraigWilson (craigwilson@gmail.com)
To: jjdawes@aol.com

Sorry for any inconvenience, I'm in a terrible situation. Am stranded here in Ukrein since last night. I was beaten and robbed on my way to the hotel I stayed and my luggage is still in custody of the hotel management pending when I make payment on outstanding bills I owe. Am waiting for my colleague to send me money to get back home but he hasn't responded. please let me know if you can help and I will refund the money back to you as soon as I get back home. My return flight will be leaving soon, please let me know if I can count on you..

Craig

 Q2 What might alert you to the fact that this was not from your friend Craig Wilson, who you may not have seen for a few months?

You should always beware of links in emails! The email is usually not addressed to you personally and often contains spelling and grammar mistakes. Sometimes it contains a threat that something bad will happen if you don't click on the link, for example, your account will be closed down in two days' time.

 Q3 Describe one other way you might recognise a 'phishing' email. How can you protect yourself from falling for a phishing attack?

Pharming

Pharming is a technique intended to redirect a website's traffic to another, fake site. The attacker will put code on your hard drive or on the actual server itself. When you type in a genuine website address, pharming redirects you to a fake/bogus website and you will be asked to give personal details.

Pharming can be carried out by changing the hosts file on the victim's computer or by exploiting a vulnerability in DNS server software. (DNS servers are the computers responsible for translating Internet names into their real IP addresses.)

Pharming is a major concern for online banking and e-commerce websites.

Shouldering

All of the above security risks are remote theft. But there are other ways to gain unauthorised access to passwords and confidential material. **Shouldering** or **shoulder-surfing** refers to using direct observation techniques to gain information such as passwords or security data; for example, looking over someone's shoulder while they type in their PIN or password.

In a crowded place such as a high street or an airport, it may be relatively easy for someone to watch you as you type in a PIN or password.

6.3 Malicious code

Security is about keeping your computer and the files, programs and data stored on it safe from a number of hazards. These hazards come in the form of malware, hackers, blagging, phishing, pharming, hardware and software faults. Other users on networks can also be one of the biggest risks of all.

Malware

Malware is the term used to refer to a variety of forms of hostile or intrusive software, some of which are described below.

Computer virus

A **virus** is a program that is installed on a computer without your knowledge or permission with the purpose of doing harm. It includes instructions to replicate (copy itself) automatically on a computer and between computers.

Some viruses are just annoying and don't really do any damage but others will delete and/or change system files so that work files are corrupted or the computer becomes unusable. Some viruses fill up the hard drive/SSD so that your computer runs very slowly or becomes unresponsive.

How are viruses spread?

- Viruses are often spread though attachment to emails or instant messaging services. You may be invited to open a funny image, greetings card, audio or video file.

- They may also be spread through files, programs or games that you download from a web page or by loading an infected file from a memory stick or a CD/DVD

> **Q4** Can a CD or DVD containing games software, bought new from a reputable manufacturer, contain a virus? Why is this unlikely?

Spyware

Spyware is software that gathers information about a person or organisation without their knowledge. It is often used to track and store users' movements on the Internet. Some spyware may change computer settings, making unauthorised changes in browser settings or changes to software settings. It can also be used to collect personal information such as user logins or bank details.

The use of the term "spyware" has declined since the practice of tracking users' visits to different websites is used by many major websites and data mining companies and is not illegal. The information gathered is commonly used in **adware** (see below).

Adware

Adware analyses which Internet sites a user visits and then presents adverts for products which the user is likely to be interested in.

Adware is sometimes integrated into free software, so that the developer can recover development costs. Advertisement-funded software is often used with open-source software, and a large number of companies will pay to have their products advertised to selected customers in this way.

Adware is also sometimes described as malware and anti-adware software is available. However, most adware operates legally and some adware manufacturers have even sued antivirus companies for blocking adware.

Trojan

A **Trojan**, named after the famous Ancient Greek story of the Trojan Horse, is a program which masquerades as having one legitimate purpose but actually has another. It is normally spread by email. The user is invited to click on a link for some routine or interesting purpose, which then executes a program which may, for example, give the controller unauthorised access to that computer. The motives vary – the Trojan may crash the computer, spread malware across the network, corrupt data or reformat disks or access sensitive information. Often these emails will purport to be from legitimate companies but contain errors and incorrect company branding as shown below.

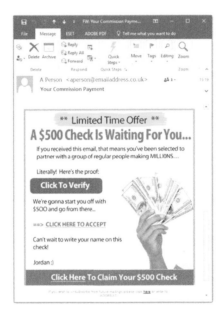

6.4 Detecting and preventing cyber security threats

Identifying vulnerabilities

There are some methods a company can use to identify vulnerabilities. These include:

- Network forensics
- Penetration testing

Network forensics

In police work, forensics often involves the use of scientific methods and techniques in investigating a crime. The term is applied in a similar way in the context of network forensics. It involves capturing, storing and analysing network events. Using special software, network managers can look at business transactions to verify that they are not fraudulent, or stop a security attack before it brings the network to a grinding halt. It can also detect data leaks, where confidential data is going to an external source.

Network forensics can reveal who communicated with whom, when, how, and how often.

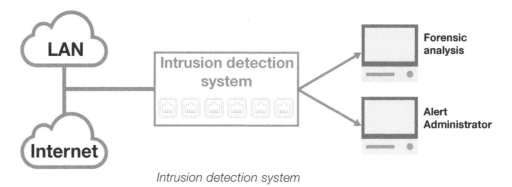

Intrusion detection system

Penetration Testing

Penetration testing is used to find any security weaknesses in a system. It attempts to gain access to resources without knowledge of usernames, passwords and other normal means of access. The strategy is to:

- gather information about the target of possible attacks
- identify possible entry points
- attempt to break in
- report back the findings

In a **black box penetration test,** testers are given very little or no information about the network prior to the test. The test could target e-mail servers, web servers or firewalls. The objective is to find out whether a hacker can get in and, once they're in, how far they can get and what they can do on the system.

In a **white box penetration test**, the tester is given basic information about the network in advance of the testing. This could include IP addresses, network protocols and even passwords. It puts the tester in the position of an insider, to determine how much damage a disgruntled or dishonest employee could cause.

> **Q5** Name some possible weaknesses or vulnerabilities that (a) a black box penetration test and (b) a white box penetration test might identify.

Preventing vulnerabilities

Anti-malware software

Anti-malware software will protect a computer in three ways:

- It prevents harmful programs from being installed on the computer
- It prevents important files, such as the operating system, from being changed or deleted
- If a virus does manage to install itself, the software will detect it when it performs regular scans. Any virus detected will be removed.

New viruses are created regularly so it is important that any antivirus software gets regular updates from the Internet.

Automatic software updates

Some popular software is a common target for malware. Browsers, pdf readers and other software can be automatically updated by selecting options to *Automatically update and install* either from the operating system or from the software. This will remove any harmful code that has been planted in the software by a hacker, or potential vulnerabilities that could be exploited in the future.

Biometric methods

Employees of an organisation or members of the public passing through airport security, for example, may be asked to identify themselves by using a **biometric method** to prove to the system that they are who they claim to be. Biometric methods include a fingerprint scan, voice pattern sample or retinal scan. The probability of two people having identical biological characteristics is infinitesimally small, and so these methods can be used to positively identify a person.

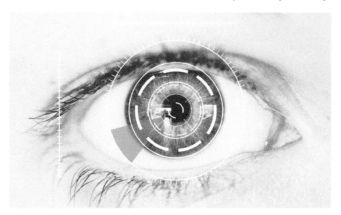

Biometric methods are often used on mobile devices. The advantage of these methods over password entry are that it is not possible to steal or forget a biometric characteristic.

CAPTCHA

CAPTCHA is an acronym for "Completely Automated Public Turing test to tell Computers and Humans Apart", and is a type of test to determine whether or not the user is human.

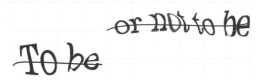

A piece of text is displayed on screen in a format indecipherable by text recognition software. Context is critical; a t might look like an **l** or **i**, and it is only in context that a human can identify it as a **t**.

> **Q6** Even perfectly sighted individuals sometimes find CAPTCHA text very difficult or impossible to read. Does the use of CAPTCHA images discriminate against any computer users?

Using email to confirm a user's identity

When you sign up to a new web service, you sometimes have to wait for a confirmation email. You will not be a registered user until you click on the link to finish the registration process and activate the account. Using email confirmations does provide some more certainty about the identity of the user.

If email confirmation is not used, and users are instead asked to enter their email address, they may give a false address as they do not wish to receive advertising emails. However, there is a problem with this – if they forget their password, there is no way to send them a new one.

From the web service's point of view, having a valid email address for everyone who registers on their site is valuable for marketing purposes. Email confirmation also prevents someone who has not registered on the site, but whose email address was given by another user, from receiving unwanted marketing emails.

To prevent this from happening, some sites will include a message with their marketing emails such as: "If you did not create an account with us and have received this email in error, please click this link."

> **Q7** Have you ever been required to wait for email confirmation and click on a link to complete a registration process? Do you always complete the registration?

Exercises

1. (a) Explain why removable media can be a threat to the security of a network. [2]

   (b) Suggest **two** ways that computer users can leave themselves open to hackers. [2]

2. (a) Explain with an example what is meant by "blagging". [2]

   (b) What measures can a company take to reduce or eliminate incidents of blagging? [1]

3. (a) What is "phishing"? [2]

   (b) Describe **two** ways that it is often possible to detect a phishing email. [2]

   (c) Explain what is meant by "shouldering". [2]

   (d) Describe **one** other way in which a criminal may obtain personal information about someone without their consent or knowledge. [2]

4. (a) What is the purpose of **penetration testing**? [1]

   (b) Describe two different types of penetration testing [4]

5. Describe **two** biometric methods of identification, and for each one, give an example of where it might be used. (Give different examples for each method.) [4]

Section 7 – Impacts of digital technology

Objectives

7

- Investigate the following issues related to Computer Science technologies:
  - o   ethical issues
  - o   legal issues
  - o   cultural issues
  - o   environmental issues
  - o   privacy issues

- Explain the risks of digital technology on society

7.1 Ethical issues

Computers have become so widespread that we cannot imagine life without them. What impact has this had on our culture? For example:

* Do we tend to ignore ethical issues in our use of computers?

* Has it become more acceptable to be rude to or bully complete strangers now that this is possible online?

* Have we become a more, or a less caring society?

 Q1 Think of some other ways in which computer technology has changed the way we live and work.

Recent developments in software

For years, computer companies have been developing software programs to take on human opponents in games such as chess. **Deep Blue** was the first chess-playing computer to beat a world champion in 1996 when it defeated Gary Kasparov, the reigning world champion.

Go is a Chinese game significantly more complex than chess, played by millions of people all over the world. It is played on a 19 x 19 grid, with one player placing black stones and the other placing white stones, the object being to control more territory than your opponent. It has long been an objective in the field of artificial intelligence (AI) to develop software to beat a human champion.

Case sudy: DeepMind AlphaGo program

In March 2016 world champion Go player Lee Se-dol from South Korea was defeated by Google's DeepMind AlphaGo program. This was the first time a computer had been able to beat a human player at the game.

The program taught itself how to improve by splitting itself in half and playing millions of matches against itself, learning from each win and loss. In one day alone, AlphaGo was able to play itself more than a million times, gaining more experience than a human player could in a lifetime.

The co-founder Demis Hassabis said he hoped to use the same technique to help Google improve its products, such as its phone assistants and search engine. The software learns by trial and error, incrementally improving and learning from its mistakes so that it makes better decisions.

The rise of artificial intelligence

Where will we go next? Science fiction is full of stories of robots that plot against their human creators and ultimately replace them.

A recent YouGov survey for the British Science Association of more than 2,000 people found that:

* 60% think that the use of robots or programs equipped with artificial intelligence (AI) will lead to fewer jobs within ten years.

* 36% of the public believe that the development of AI poses a threat to the long term survival of humanity.

- Generally, people don't trust robots to take on roles where their lives could be in danger. Respondents would not trust robots to carry out surgical procedures (53%), drive public buses (49%) or fly commercial aircraft (62%).

- 13% of men, but only 6% of women, thought they could be friends with a robot.

- 28% of 18-24 year-olds thought that robots could be future co-workers and ten per cent imagined that they could regard them as family members.

Q2   What do you think about these issues? What are your reasons in each case? What are the cultural issues involved here?

Driverless cars

Robots are being used to replace humans in many occupations. They do not necessarily look like a human. For example, Google's driverless cars are already being tested on Britain's roads. But what of the legal issues? Will the car be able to distinguish between a fox, a child and a plastic bag and make the appropriate decision about what action to take?

If someone is hurt or killed by a driverless car, who is to blame? The manufacturer, the owner of the car, or the person in charge of the car at the time?

Q3   What are the benefits and drawbacks of driverless cars?

7

Designer babies

Computers have enabled our entire genetic code to be mapped. This has led to extraordinary advances in medicine but has also raised ethical issues.

It is possible for prospective parents who have an inherited abnormality or disease to opt for genetic screening of embryos prior to implantation, so that a baby is highly likely to be free of the disease under consideration. In some cases, the term "designer baby" refers to the proposed use of pre-implantation genetic diagnosis to select desired traits for the child such as gender, hair colour, height, athletic ability or intelligence. Is this an ethical use of digital technology?

Social networking

Many people of all ages use social networking sites and Twitter to keep in touch with friends and family. If you are out and about, you are more likely to post a photograph and a comment on Facebook than send a postcard. You can communicate with friends and family all over the world very easily.

As well as keeping in touch, people use Internet dating sites to meet people rather than going to bars and clubs. Social networking using computer technology has become normal. Some people think this is great because you can have more 'friends' but others think we are losing the ability to socially interact face-to-face.

Digital exposure carries risks. A recent survey by Parent Zone revealed that although 74.5% of teenagers report that the Internet made them happy, 36% admitted they would suggest friends avoid Facebook if they were feeling worried or upset.

Q4 What are the dangers of social networking sites such as Facebook? What are the benefits?

The rating culture

Using a mobile phone, you can keep in constant touch with all your friends. You can make new "friends", and find out a lot about them. You can use your phone to find your way around, check out the look of a place you are going to visit, book a cinema ticket, a holiday or a taxi ride.

You can then rate people, places and events, giving them a score based on what you thought of them. Let's look more closely at this practice.

On the face of it, being able to look at the average rating of a film, book, restaurant or holiday destination seems a very helpful idea. But it can go further than that.

Case study: Rating taxi drivers

When you book a taxi through Uber, for example, you can rate the driver. Passengers are essentially unpaid supervisors of the company, monitoring drivers' behaviour so that Uber can manage its workforce. The passengers have quite a lot of power here – if an Uber driver's score dips below 4.6 out of 5 they may get "deactivated" and no longer drive for Uber. But a lot of people might consider that 4.6 out of 5 is a very good score.

So what is a driver being scored on? Type of car is a big factor. Uber suggests that drivers should offer water to the passengers. Really? If the driver can't find that little pub in a back street of a big city where you're meeting your friends, do you give him or her a bad score?

And don't forget, as a passenger, the driver can rate you, too.

Q5 What factors would you take into consideration when rating an Uber taxi driver?

Rating goes far beyond Uber. There are apps that let you rate your co-workers, your teachers, pupils and bosses. The Peeple app launched in March 2016 lets you rate other people, "Revolutionising the way we're seen in the world, through our relationships." You can rate anyone you come in contact with in three ways – personally, professionally and romantically – provided you allow yourself to be "recommended" by others.

Q6 Does this get you better job opportunities, better dates, better networking opportunities? What are the upsides, downsides and dangers of using a site like this? Can humans be rated?

Q7 Do some research on the Internet and find out more about these two applications.

Risks of digital technology

- In-car satellite-navigation systems are commonly programmed to find the quickest route to your destination. Is it ethical to program a route to a popular destination which takes a multitude of drivers through a previously quiet, safe residential neighbourhood where there may be children playing outside?

- There is an obvious danger posed by the fact that a simple 3D print file can be downloaded from the Internet and a gun fabricated within hours. Should there be a blanket ban on sharing such files? Is it even possible to impose such a ban?

7.2 Digital technology in society

Computer technology impacts just about everything we do. What are the risks to society of the ever-increasing use of digital technology?

Here are a few areas to consider.

Employment

Computer technology has had a huge impact on employment. Many types of work have disappeared, and new jobs have been created.

Computer technology has already led to the loss of thousands of different jobs, for example in:

- clerical work
- manufacturing and
- the photographic industry.

Robots could soon surpass humans in routine legal work, language translation and medical diagnosis – but plumbers, gardeners and physiotherapists will be hard to replace.

Thousands of new jobs have been created as a result of computer technology:

- software and hardware development
- creation of a multitude of new products from robots, "smart homes" and mobile technologies to online learning materials and aids for disabled people.

Q8 Name **three** jobs that you think could be computerised, and **five** jobs that cannot easily be computerised.

Shopping

Online shopping has led to the closing of many High Street stores.

It has also helped people who find it difficult to get to a supermarket for their food shopping, or to shops to buy any of the thousands of other items now readily available online.

7 Computers in healthcare

Computers plays a hugely important role in healthcare. As well as the administrative tasks that computers perform, they are used for example to monitor patients, administer drugs, and diagnose illnesses. There are now more than 165,000 health-related apps which run on one or other of the two main smart-phone operating systems, Apple's iOS and Google's Android.

These apps will have been downloaded 1.7 billion times by 2017. Check out, for example, **your.MD** online to see how one of these apps works.

As these apps become more popular, there are concerns that some health apps may be sharing patients' health data without their knowledge.

Q9 What sort of data might be shared? Who would it be shared with, and how could this impact an individual?

Computer-aided diagnosis is being used to improve diagnosis and treatment.

These tools need to be scrutinised ethically as well as scientifically or economically; would we be happy with a diagnostic tool that saved lives overall but discriminated against some patients? Who is responsible for computer-based decisions in healthcare?

Q10 It has been suggested that computers could replace human beings in healthcare decision-making. Discuss the cultural and ethical issues involved in such a scenario.

Computer-based implants

Computer-based implants have been used in many different fields of medicine:

- Cochlear implants have been successful in restoring partial hearing to profoundly deaf people

- Heart implants may include electrodes for regulating heartbeat, warn of heart attacks and monitor the effects of treatment

- Recently a quadriplegic man, Erik Sorto, had electrodes implanted in his brain which enable him to control a robotic arm, getting it to bring a cup to his mouth simply by thinking about doing it.

Risks of computer-based implants

Many implanted devices need to be capable of being reprogrammed, and they have to collect monitoring data from the patients which can be read by medical staff. Theoretically, it is possible for a malicious person to hack into an implanted device and collect data illegally, or even to reprogram it to harm or kill the patient.

Wearable technologies

The latest wearable technologies include items that can:

- be worn as a wristwatch and monitor your movements, number of steps, time spent sleeping, sitting or standing and then tell you "how to live better"

- be worn by a swimmer, attached to swimming goggles on the back of the head and measure kick-turn times, breath counts and stroke efficiency

- tighten your trainers around your feet automatically at the touch of a button, like Nike's replica Marty McFly's Mag trainers.

Some of these devices, as well as your mobile phone, enable your movements to be tracked by your friends and family, or by complete strangers without your knowledge.

 Q11 Does the thought of someone tracking your movements without your knowledge worry you? In what ways can this technology be useful to society?

Environmental impact of computers

Environmental issues include the carbon footprint and waste products that result from manufacturing computer systems, but these are often outweighed by the positive effects on the environment of using computerised systems to manage processes that might otherwise generate more pollution.

Considerations may include:

- Does a computer system mean that people can work from home and therefore drive less?

- Has computer technology led to a "throw-away society", with huge waste dumps of unwanted products which are thrown away rather than repaired or upgraded?

- Is working at home more environmentally friendly than everyone working in a big office, in terms of shared heating and lighting?

- Do computer-managed engines work more efficiently, create less pollution and use less fuel?

Wireless networking

Wireless networking is being used in the development of 'smart cities', with technology being used to improve the running of urban areas. This includes everything from identifying which roads need gritting when it snows, to controlling smart streetlights.

Streetlights have traditionally been turned on and off by sensors. Using wireless technology, nodes attached to each streetlight can communicate with base stations up to five miles away. The base stations in turn communicate with the controller and the authorities can manipulate the lights as they want. They can be dimmed at certain times in particular areas to save energy, and ascertain when a streetlight is not working so that it can be rapidly fixed.

About 10% of the UK's 7m street lights are fitted with smart technology, with networks consisting of 10,000 lights or more. A project in Doncaster estimates that the technology will save them £1.3m each year from reduced energy consumption.

There are risks associated with highly connected systems, including technical failure which could disrupt the entire network of streetlights. Cyber-security threats are always an issue; if someone with malicious intent gained access to the system, they could potentially disrupt the lighting in a particular area so that for example it was completely unlit, for whatever reason.

Computers and waste

The pace of technology is so rapid that computers, mobile phones and handheld-devices that seemed so desirable a few short years ago are now discarded without a thought for the latest must-have piece of equipment. Are they recyclable or are they simply contributing to a huge mountain of waste, containing dangerous chemical elements which leach into water supplies in third-world countries?

Computer-aided manufacturing can result in more and cheaper products. But does this lead to more waste? Disposable coffee cups used in their millions every day by people at work are cheap to make, thanks to modern technology. They are made from paper laminated with plastic, and so are largely unrecyclable. Three billion coffee cups were handed out last year in coffee shops in the UK, and fewer than one in 400 was recycled.

Q12 Think of some ways in which computers have helped to decrease environmental pollution, by monitoring the environment or by replacing old polluting industries with more environmentally friendly products, for example in the energy industry.

Monitoring the environment

Computers are widely used for monitoring the environment. Water quality in rivers and oceans, air quality in cities, pollen levels in the countryside which affect people with hay fever and asthma, radiation in nuclear plants, can all be monitored and warnings given.

Data which helps to predict earthquakes, tsunamis, hurricanes and other natural disasters is collected and analysed continuously all over the world. Weather data can be collected from the top of a mountain or from inside a volcano without a scientist having to go into these dangerous situations every day to collect it

Using data collected about weather, volcanic activity, and movement beneath the earth's surface, people can be warned about impending disasters such as hurricanes and earthquakes, and moved to safety.

7.3 Legislation and privacy

Legal issues

The law can affect the way that computer systems are developed, how they are used and how they are disposed of, for example.

The Data Protection Act 1998

The Data Protection Act says that anyone who stores personal details must keep them secure. Companies with computer systems that store any personal data must have processes and security mechanisms designed into the system to meet this requirement.

The act includes a number of principles:

- data must be processed fairly and lawfully
- data must be adequate, relevant and not excessive
- data must be accurate and up to date
- data must not be retained for longer than necessary
- data can only be used for the purpose for which it was collected
- data must be kept secure
- data must be handled in accordance with people's rights
- data must not be transferred outside of the EU without adequate protection

You do not need to remember the individual clauses of the Act given above, but you need to consider the implications of this legislation. For example, it is illegal to pass on or sell details of customers who have bought items from you, to another organisation without their permission. Organisations must make sure that the data they hold is accurate. Inaccurate data about a person's credit rating, for example, can have very serious consequences for an individual. Muddling one person's data with another can wreak havoc with an individual's life.

> **Q13** An accountant's practice were found to have thrown old customer records from 2005 in the waste bins outside their offices. Which principles of the Act may have been broken?

The Computer Misuse Act 1990

The Computer Misuse Act has three main principles, primarily designed to prevent unauthorised access or 'hacking' of programs or data.

The Computer Misuse Act (1990) recognised the following new offences:

- Unauthorised access to computer material
- Unauthorised access with intent to commit or facilitate a crime
- Unauthorised modification of computer material
- Making, supplying or obtaining anything which can be used in computer misuse offences.

Again, you do not need to memorise the clauses of the Act, but you should be able to identify it as the Act which, for example, makes hacking illegal.

7

> **Q14** Describe some other behaviours which would be illegal under this Act.

The Copyright Designs and Patents Act 1988

This Act is designed to protect the creators of books, music, video and software from having their work illegally copied.

The Act makes it illegal to use, copy or distribute commercially available software without buying the appropriate licence. When a computer system is designed and implemented, licensing must be considered in terms of which software should be used.

If you buy a music CD or pay to download a piece of music, software or a video, it is illegal to:

- pass a copy to a friend
- make a copy and then sell it
- use the software on a network, unless the licence allows it.

However, although a piece of software such as an applications package, game or operating system is protected, **algorithms** are not eligible for protection. If you come up with a much better sorting algorithm than anyone else, you cannot stop others from using it.

For a song writer, having their work illegally copied has the same effect as stealing money from them. The same is true of copying software illegally; software can take years to develop and involve hundreds of people. Individuals and software companies, whether large or small, cannot afford to have their work stolen.

Privacy issues

It is predicted that small computers will become embedded in everything from clothes to beermats. Consequently, we will be interfacing with computers in everything we do, from meeting chip-wearing strangers to entering smart buildings or sitting on a smart sofa, and each of these interfaces will end up on a Google database.

It is a vision of a world without privacy.

Already, Google collects and stores data about millions of emails every day. Here are some extracts from the information they post on their website, which users must agree to if they wish to use Google software.

To be consistent with data protection laws, we're asking you to take a moment to review key points of Google's Privacy Policy. This isn't about a change that we've made - it's just a chance to review some key points.

Data we process when you use Google

- When you search for a restaurant on Google Maps or watch a video on YouTube, for example, we process information about the activity - including information like the video you watched, device IDs, IP addresses, cookie data and location.
- We also process the kind of information described above when you use apps or sites that use Google services like ads, Analytics and the YouTube video player.

Why we process it

We process this data for the purposes described in our policy, including to:

- Help our services deliver more useful, customised content such as more relevant search results;
- Improve the quality of our services and develop new ones;
- Deliver ads based on your interests, including things like searches you've done or videos you've watched on YouTube;
- Improve security by protecting against fraud and abuse; and
- Conduct analytics and measurement to understand how our services are used.

7

Organisations including governments and security agencies, collect huge amounts of data about private citizens, often supplied by Internet companies such as Google, as well as telephone companies.

With the aim of detecting terrorist or other illegal activities, the US Government collects, stores and monitors metadata about all electronic communications in the US. **Metadata** includes information such as the telephone number called, date, time and duration of call.

In one month in 2013, the unit collected data on more than 97 billion emails and 124 billion phone calls from around the world. Edward Snowden is a famous 'whistle-blower' who informed the world about these practices.

Q15 Why do some people object to this data being collected and stored? What are the arguments for and against organisations collecting such data?

Using cookies

Cookies are files, often including unique identifiers, that are sent by web servers to web browsers, and which may then be sent back to the server each time the browser requests a page from the server.

They are used:

- to recognise your computer when you visit the website

- to track you as you navigate the website, and to enable the use of any e-commerce facilities

- to improve the website's usability

- to analyse the use of the website

- in the administration of the website

- to personalise the website for you, including targeting advertisements which may be of particular interest to you.

Some websites remind you that they will collect data about you:

Hacking

In May 2015, a computer security expert flying on a passenger airliner hacked into the aircraft's computer controls through the entertainment system and briefly made it fly sideways. He told the FBI he did this to demonstrate the vulnerabilities in the computer system so that they would be fixed.

The prospect of an aircraft being brought down by a hacker rather than a bomb, which has to pass through security and be placed on board, is a new and unwelcome possibility!

Case study: Hacking into smart meters

GCHQ, the British Government intelligence and security organisation, has intervened in the design of an £11bn nationwide system of smart meters to secure them against attempts by hackers to crash the country's power grids. The agency discovered loopholes in the system that it believes could pose a national security threat by causing a collapse in the national grid system by potentially gaining control of every meter.

The meters automatically send readings back to the energy suppliers instead of the householder or an employee of the energy company having to read gas and electricity meters. The new metering system is one of the biggest IT projects in a generation. Energy companies have already installed about two million of the 53 million smart meters due to be installed across the country by 2020.

Exercises

1. Some governments and security services may collect data about all telephone calls and email communications made by their citizens. This may amount to several billion records every month. They argue that they cannot keep their citizens safe from terrorism unless they have access to private data.

    Do you agree that they should be allowed to do this? Give arguments in support of and against this practice.   [5]

2. Michael's main job is working for a company, called *SekureSoft*, which develops and then sells software used by security companies. However, in the evening he works with a small team to write his own games software.

    Look at the following statements and decide whether each can be regarded as an ethical issue, a legal issue or a cultural issue. (It is possible that some statements fall into none, or more than one, of these categories.) Justify your answer in each case.

    a.   Michael uses some of the software he develops for *SekureSoft* in his own games software

    b.   Michael employs people in India and China to write routines for his games software; he pays them a very low wage to do this work

    c.   Some of the games software that Michael writes has features which are difficult for people with certain disabilities to use

    d.   Whilst working through the day at *SekureSoft*, Michael sometimes uses their very powerful computer systems to test out some of the routines he uses in his games software

    e.   Michael hires a hacker to break into websites of certain companies to allow him to advertise his games software free of charge using "pop ups"

    f.   Michael has included routines in the software he writes for *SekureSoft* that feed back information from security companies that buy their software; this feedback is used to help make his computer games more realistic.   [12]

7

Index

I

Lightning Source UK Ltd.
Milton Keynes UK
UKOW07f0616120616

276098UK00007B/13/P